Q̲u̲...̲...̲e̲

MW01473012

(DDC)

WordPerfect®
for Windows™
Versions 5.1 & 5.2

Marivel Salazar/Angelo Cassano

(DDC)
Dictation Disc Company
14 East 38 Street, New York, NY 10016

First Dictation Disc Printing

Cat.# Z-17

ISBN: 1-56243-061-0

10   9   8   7   6   5   4   3

Printed in the United States of America

INTRODUCTION

The **DDC Quick Reference Guide for WordPerfect 5.1/5.2 for Windows** will save you hours of searching through technical manuals.

A template for the WordPerfect CUA (Common User Access) compatible keyboard layout is illustrated on the outside back cover. A template for the WordPerfect DOS-compatible keyboard layout is illustrated on the inside back cover. When installing WordPerfect for Windows you will be asked which keyboard layout you will be using. You can change the keyboard layout at any time (see Select a Keyboard Layout on page 136).

Before You Begin

You should be familiar with basic cursor movements (see Insertion Point Movements on page 134) and highlighting procedures (see Select Text on pages 218-221).

Mouse users can select menu options by placing the insertion point on an item and clicking the left mouse button. For further information on selecting items with a mouse, (see Select Dialog Box Items on pages 214-217).

Authors
Marivel Salazar
Angelo Cassano
Karl Schwartz

Technical Editors
Joanne Schwartz
Paul Berube
Marianne Merola

Editors
Mike Church
Kathy Berkemeyer

Special Acknowledgments
Maria Reidlbach
Adrienne Plotch

TABLE OF CONTENTS

Continued ...

TABLE OF CONTENTS (continued)

Continued ...

iv

TABLE OF CONTENTS (continued)

ADVANCE

Advances text to an exact location on a page. Use Advance to place text in a fill-in form or graphics box, for example.

1. Place insertion point where advance will begin.
2. Select **L**ayout menu . . . . **Alt** + **L**
3. Select **A**dvance . . . . **A**
4. Select desired advance option . . . . **letter**
   U̲p, D̲own, To L̲ine, L̲eft, R̲ight, To P̲osition
5. Select **A**dvance text box . . . . **A**
6. Type distance (inches) to advance . . . . **number**
   NOTE: If you selected U̲p, D̲own, L̲eft, or R̲ight, specify a distance relative to the current position. If you selected L̲ine, specify a distance from the top edge of the page. If you selected P̲osition, specify a distance from the left edge of the page.
7. Select **OK** . . . . **↵**
   NOTE: If you selected L̲ine or U̲p, the result will not show on the screen. See PRINT PREVIEW (page 188) to view document as it will appear when printed.

APPEND

Append to Clipboard

Adds selected text or graphics to the end of existing data in the Clipboard.

1. Select text (page 218) or graphics box (page 95).
   NOTE: Tabular Columns, or rectangles cannot be appended to Clipboard. If the Clipboard contains tabular columns or rectangles that have been cut or copied, text or graphics cannot be appended.
2. Select **E**dit menu . . . . **Alt** + **E**
3. Select Appen**d** . . . . **D**
4. Repeat steps 1-3 for each piece of data to append.

2

Append to File

Adds selected text (and any graphics within text selection) to the end of an existing file.

1. Select text (page 218) to append to file.
2. Select File menu . . . . 【Alt】+【F】
3. Select Save . . . . 【S】
4. Select file to append to in Files list box . . 【Alt】+【I】, 【¼】
   See DIRECTORIES — LOCATING FILES, page 25.
5. Select Save . . . . 【↵】
6. Select Append . . . . 【A】

AUTO CODE PLACEMENT ON/OFF

Places certain formatting codes at the top of page or beginning of paragraph regardless of insertion point location. The code remains in effect until the same type of formatting code is encountered. If Auto Code Placement is off, the codes inserted affect text from insertion point forward, until the same formatting code is encountered.

1. Select File menu . . . . 【Alt】+【F】
2. Select Preferences . . . . 【E】
3. Select Environment . . . . 【E】
4. Select or clear □Auto Code Placement . . . . 【P】
5. Select OK . . . . 【↵】

BACKUP

Timed Document Backup protects against losing data due to power interruption or systems failure (crashes). Documents are automatically saved to a temporary backup file at specified intervals. When WordPerfect is exited, all Timed Document Backup files are deleted.

*Original Document Backup saves a copy of the original document before most recent editing changes to a file that contains the same name as the file, but has a .BK! extension. **Example:** Filename.BK!*

Set Document Backup Options

1. Select File menu .... `Alt` + `F`
2. Select Preferences .... `E`
3. Select Backup .... `B`
4. Select ☐Original Document Backup .... `O`

   NOTE: *Recover all original backup files before clearing Original Document Backup option. If the option is cleared, the next time you save a document, any backup of the same name is deleted.*

   AND/OR   **AND/OR**

   Select ☐Timed Document Backup .... `T`

   a) Select increment box .... `Tab`
   b) Type number of minutes between backups ... **number**
5. Select **OK** .... `⏎`

Recover Original Document Backup Files

1. Open backup document file (page 167).

   NOTE: *Backup files have the same name as edited documents but have .BK! extensions.*
   ***Example:** Filename.BK!*
2. Save file with new name (page 212).

   NOTE: *Do not use a BK! filename extension.*

4

Recover Timed Document Backup Files

1. Restart WordPerfect.

   When WordPerfect discovers that a timed document backup file exists, the Timed dialog box appears.

   FROM TIMED DIALOG BOX

2. Select one option:

   - **R**ename .... $\boxed{\text{R}}$

     a) Type a filename .... **filename**

     b) Select **OK** .... $\boxed{\text{↵}}$

   - **O**pen .... $\boxed{\text{O}}$
     to edit or save Timed Document Backup File.

   - **D**elete .... $\boxed{\text{D}}$

   NOTE: Timed Document Backup files are deleted when you exit WordPerfect properly.

BEEP ON/OFF

Sets your computer to beep when specified conditions or errors occur.

1. Select **F**ile menu .... $\boxed{\text{Alt}}$ + $\boxed{\text{F}}$

2. Select Pr**e**ferences .... $\boxed{\text{E}}$

3. Select **E**nvironment .... $\boxed{\text{E}}$

4. Select or clear desired option(s) in
   Beep On group .... $\boxed{\text{Alt}}$ + **letter**

   Error, Hyphenation, Search Failure

5. Select **OK** .... $\boxed{\text{↵}}$

BLOCK PROTECT

Prevents selected text from being split by a soft page break.

1. Select text (page 218) to protect from soft page break.

2. Select **L**ayout menu .... `Alt` + `L`

3. Select **P**age .... `P`

4. Select **B**lock Protect .... `B`

BOLD

Bolds existing text or bolds text as it is typed.

1. Select text (page 218) to bold.

   OR

   Place insertion point where boldfaced text will begin.

2. Select F**o**nt menu .... `Alt` + `O`

3. Select **B**old .... `B`

   If text was selected,

   • Press **Right** arrow to deselect text .... `→`

   If text was not selected,

   a) Type text .... text

   b) Repeat steps 2 and 3 to turn bold off.

BUTTON BAR

Use mouse to access frequently used commands and macros.

Display/Remove Button Bar

1. Select **V**iew menu .... `Alt` + `V`

2. Select or deselect **B**utton Bar .... `B`

NOTE: WordPerfect will display the last Button Bar you selected.

BUTTON BAR (continued)

Select Button on Button Bar

NOTE: *If the Button Bar is filled, directional arrows appear*
*on the Button Bar. Click on **Left** or **Right Arrow** to*
scroll to buttons that are not visible.

• Click on desired button on Button Bar.

Select a Button Bar

Switch between existing Button Bars.

1. Point anywhere on Button Bar
   <u>and</u> click right mouse button. (*WP5.2*)

2. Click on name of desired Button Bar.

OR

1. Click on . . . . V̲iew

2. Click on . . . . Button Bar S̲etup

3. Click on . . . . S̲elect

4. Click on desired filename in F̲iles list box.

5. Click on . . . . S̲elect

Create or Edit Button Bar

1. Click on . . . . V̲iew

2. Click on . . . . Button Bar S̲etup

   Mouse shortcut: (*WP5.2*) Steps 1 and 2: Point anywhere
   on Button Bar <u>and</u> click right mouse
   button.

3. Click on . . . . N̲ew
   OR   **OR**
   Click on . . . . E̲dit

Continued ...

BUTTON BAR — Create or Edit Button Bar (continued)

4. Add, move, delete, or assign macros to buttons as desired:

   To <u>add</u> button to button bar:

   a) Click on desired menu.
      Mouse pointer becomes a 🖑 *when placed on menu bar.*

   b) Click on desired menu item(s) until button is placed on Button Bar.

   c) Repeat steps a and b for each button to add.

   To <u>move</u> button on button bar:

   • Drag desired button to new position on Button Bar.
     Mouse pointer becomes a 🖑 *when placed on a button.*

   To <u>delete</u> button from button bar:

   • Drag desired button off Button Bar.
     Mouse pointer becomes a 🖑 *when placed on a button.*

   To <u>assign</u> macro to a button:

   a) Click on . . . . `Assign Macro to Button...`

   b) Click on desired filename in <u>F</u>iles list box.

   c) Click on . . . . `Assign...`

   NOTE: *A macro assigned to a button can not be edited.*
   A new button for edited macro must be added or
   the button must be deleted before editing macro.

5. Click on . . . . `OK`
   to save changes.

   If creating a new Button Bar,

   a) Type a filename in Save <u>A</u>s text box . . . . . . **filename**

   b) Click on . . . . `Save`

NOTE: *If the Button Bar is filled, directional arrows appear on*
the Button Bar. Click on **Left** *or* **Right Arrow** *to scroll to*
buttons that are not visible.

BUTTON BAR (continued)

Change Position and Appearance of Button Bar

NOTE: Changes made will affect all Button Bars.

1. Point anywhere on Button Bar
   <u>and</u> click the right mouse button. (*WP5.2*)

   OR

   Click on .... **View**

   • Click on .... **Button Bar Setup**

2. Click on .... **Options**

3. Click on desired position for button bar:
   Left, Right, Top, Bottom

   AND/OR

   Click on desired style (Appearance) of button bar:
   Text Only, Picture Only, Picture and Text

4. Click on .... | OK |

Rename Button Bar

1. Click on .... **View**

2. Click on .... **Button Bar Setup**

3. Click on .... **Save As**

4. Type a filename in Save As text box .... **filename**

5. Click on .... | Save |

CAPITALIZATION

Turn Caps Lock On or Off

1. Press **Caps Lock** (Upper Case on) .... | Caps Lock |
   "Pos" changes to "POS" on status line.

2. Type text .... **text**

3. Press **Caps Lock** (Upper Case off) .... | Caps Lock |
   "POS" changes back to "Pos" on status line.

CASE CONVERSION

Changes an existing block of text to all upper or lower case.

1. Select text (page 218) to convert.
2. Select Edit menu .... `Alt`+`E`
3. Select Convert Case (*WP5.2*) .... `V`

   OR   **OR**

   Select Convert Case (*WP5.1*) .... `O`
4. Select Uppercase .... `U`

   OR   **OR**

   Select Lowercase .... `L`

CENTER

Also see JUSTIFICATION on page 135.

Center Text

Centers existing text or centers text as it is typed.

1. Place insertion point where centering will begin.
2. Select Layout menu .... `Alt`+`L`
3. Select Line .... `L`
4. Select Center .... `C`
5. If desired, type text (maximum one line) .... **text**

NOTE: *You can center more than once on a line as long as text is separated by a tab or more than one space.*

End Centering/Alignment

Ends centering in the middle of a line to allow text to be typed on the same line.

1. Select Layout menu .... `Alt`+`L`
2. Select Line .... `L`
3. Select Special Codes .... `O`
4. Select ○ End Centering/Alignment .... `/`
5. Select Insert .... `I`

10

CENTER (continued)

Center Text with Dot Leader

Centers text and inserts a dot leader from starting point to beginning of centered text.

1. Place insertion point where centering will begin.
2. Select **L**ayout menu . . . . `Alt` + `L`
3. Select **L**ine . . . . `L`
4. Select **C**enter . . . . `C`
5. Repeat steps 2-4 to add dot leader.
6. If desired, type text to center . . . . **text**

Center Text on Next Tab Stop

1. Select **L**ayout menu . . . . `Alt` + `L`
2. Select **L**ine . . . . `L`
3. Select Special C**o**des . . . . `O`
4. Select ○ **C**enter [HdCntrTab] . . . . `C`
   to center over tab stop.

   OR   **OR**

   Select ○ Ce**n**ter [HdCntrTab] . . . . `N`
   to center over tab stop and add dot leader.
5. Select **I**nsert . . . . `↵`

Center Page (Top to Bottom)

1. Place insertion point at top page to center.
2. Select **L**ayout menu . . . . `Alt` + `L`
3. Select **P**age . . . . `P`
4. Select **C**enter Page . . . . `C`

NOTE: You must preview (page 188) or print (page 184) to see results of this procedure.

CLOSE

Close Document or View Windows
Closes document windows in WordPerfect; view windows in File Manager.

- Double-click on document or view window's .... `⊟`

  OR

  Select **F**ile menu in WordPerfect .... `Alt`+`F`

  - Select **C**lose .... `C`

If Save Changes to Document message box appears,

- Select **N**o .... `N`
  to close document without saving changes.

  OR   **OR**

  Select **Y**es .... `Y`
  to save document.

  a) Type a filename in Save **A**s text box .... **filename**
     NOTE: If necessary, type a path.
  b) Select **S**ave .... `↵`

Close (Exit) WordPerfect or File Manager

- Double-click on application window's .... `⊟`

  OR

  Select **F**ile menu .... `Alt`+`F`

  - Select E**x**it .... `X`

If Save Changes to Document message box appears,

a) Select **N**o .... `N`
   to exit WordPerfect without saving changes.

   OR   **OR**

   Select **Y**es .... `Y`
   to save changes and exit WordPerfect.

   1) Type a filename in Save **A**s text box .... **filename**
      NOTE: If necessary, type a path.
   2) Select **S**ave .... `↵`

b) Repeat step a for each open document.

12

COLUMNS

NOTE: *Also see RULER (pages 208-211) for information about using a mouse to create and adjust columns.*

Define and Turn On Columns

1. Place insertion point where columns will begin.

2. Select **L**ayout menu . . . . `Alt` + `L`

3. Select **C**olumns . . . . `C`

4. Select **D**efine . . . . `D`

5. Type number of columns in
   Number of **C**olumns text box . . . . **number**

   NOTE: *WordPerfect automatically calculates margin settings based on the number of columns. Maximum number of columns is 24.*

6. Select desired column type:

   ○ **N**ewspaper . . . . `Alt` + `N`
   Text flows down from bottom of one
   column to top of next column.

   ○ **P**arallel . . . . `Alt` + `P`
   Short blocks of text forming rows
   of text placed side by side.

   ○ Parallel **B**lock Protect . . . . `Alt` + `B`
   Protects parallel column rows of text
   from being split by a page break.

   To set distance between columns:

   a) Select **D**istance Between Columns text box . . `Alt` + `D`

   b) Type distance (inches) between columns . . . . **number**

   To set columns of unequal margins:

   a) Select desired Left or Right
   Margins text box . . . . `Alt` + `M`, `Tab`

   b) Type margin position . . . . **number**

   c) Repeat steps a and b for each margin to change.

Continued ...

COLUMNS — Define and Turn On Columns (continued)

To set columns of equal margins:

- Select ☐ Evenly Space . . . . `Alt`+`E`

7. Select ☐ Columns On . . . . `Alt`+`O`

8. Select OK to save changes . . . . `↵`

Turn Column Off/On

NOTE: *You must define columns (page 12) before you can turn columns on.*

1. Select Layout menu . . . . `Alt`+`L`

2. Select Columns . . . . `C`

3. Select Columns Off . . . . `F`

   OR   **OR**

   Select Columns On . . . . `O`

Column Display On/Off

Displays columns on a separate page or side by side.

1. Select File menu . . . . `Alt`+`F`

2. Select Preferences . . . . `E`

3. Select Display . . . . `D`

4. Select or clear ☐ Display Columns Side by Side . . `Alt`+`C`

5. Select OK . . . . `↵`

Convert Tables into Parallel Columns

Converts all tables in document to parallel columns.

1. Select File menu . . . . `Alt`+`F`

2. Select Save As . . . . `A`

3. Type a filename in Save As text box, if formatted file will be a new document . . . . **filename**

4. Open Format list box `↓` . . . . `Alt`+`F`, `F4`

5. Select WordPerfect 5.0 . . . . `¼`, `F4`

6. Select Save . . . . `↵`

NOTE: *Close original file and open saved file to view converted table.*

14

Insert a Column Break

Ends text in one column and moves insertion point and any text after the insertion point to next column.

1. Place insertion point where desired.

2. Press **Ctrl + Enter** (Hard Page) . . . . `Ctrl` + `⏎`

Delete a Column Break

- Delete desired [HPg] code.

  See DELETE CODES on page 23.

Move between Columns with Keyboard

Previous Column . . . . `Alt` + `←`

Next Column . . . . `Alt` + `→`

Move between Columns with Mouse

- Click in desired column.

Move between Columns using Go To

See Go To Column or Position in Column on page 58.

COMMENTS

NOTE: *Comments appear in shaded box in document, but are not printed.*

Create Comment

1. Place insertion point where comment will appear.

   NOTE: *You cannot add a comment in a column.*

2. Select <u>T</u>ools menu .... `Alt` + `T`

3. Select <u>C</u>omment (*WP5.2*) .... `C`

   OR   **OR**

   Select Comme<u>n</u>t (*WP5.1*) .... `N`

4. Select <u>C</u>reate .... `C`

5. Type comment .... **text**

   NOTE: *To enter a hard return press **Ctrl** + **Enter**.*

6. As needed, select desired attribute(s) ...... `Alt` + **letter**

   <u>B</u>old, <u>U</u>nderline, <u>I</u>talic

   NOTE: *To turn an attribute off, select it again.*

7. Select **OK** .... `⏎`

Edit Comment

1. Double-click on comment box to edit.

   OR

   Place insertion point anywhere after comment to edit.

   a) Select <u>T</u>ools menu .... `Alt` + `T`

   b) Select <u>C</u>omment (*WP5.2*) .... `C`

      OR   **OR**

   Select Comme<u>n</u>t (*WP5.1*) .... `N`

   c) Select <u>E</u>dit .... `E`

2. Edit comment.

3. Select **OK** .... `⏎`

16

Delete Comment

• Delete desired [Comment] code.
   See DELETE CODES on page 23.

Display/Hide Comments

1. Select <u>V</u>iew menu . . . . `Alt`+`V`
2. Select or deselect Comme<u>n</u>ts . . . . `N`

Convert Text to Comment

1. Select text (page 218) to convert.
2. Select <u>T</u>ools menu . . . . `Alt`+`T`
3. Select <u>C</u>omment (*WP5.2*) . . . . `C`
   OR   **OR**
   Select Comme<u>n</u>t (*WP5.1*) . . . . `N`
4. Select <u>C</u>reate . . . . `C`

Convert Comment to Text

1. If necessary, turn Reveal Codes on . . . . `Alt`+`F3`
2. Place highlight after [Comment] code.
3. Select <u>T</u>ools menu . . . . `Alt`+`T`
4. Select <u>C</u>omment (*WP5.2*) . . . . `C`
   OR   **OR**
   Select Comme<u>n</u>t (*WP5.1*) . . . . `N`
5. Select Convert to <u>T</u>ext . . . . `T`

CONDITIONAL END OF PAGE

Protects a specific number of lines from being split by a page break.

1. Place insertion point on line above text to keep together.

2. Select Layout menu .... `Alt` + `L`

3. Select Page .... `P`

4. Select Conditional End of Page .... `E`

5. Type number of lines to keep together in text box . **number**

6. Select OK .... `↵`

CONVERT DOCUMENT FILES

NOTE: *It is good practice to make a backup copy of a document prior to conversion in the event the conversion does not work well.*

Convert WordPerfect for Windows Document to Another Format

1. Select File menu .... `Alt` + `F`

2. Select Save As .... `A`

3. Type a filename in Save As text box .... **filename**

4. Open Format `▼` .... `Alt` + `F`, `F4`

5. Select desired file format .... `↕`, `F4`

6. Select Save .... `↵`

18

Convert File to WordPerfect for Windows Format

1. Select File menu . . . . `Alt`+`F`
2. Select Open . . . . `O`
3. Select desired file in Files list box . . . . `Alt`+`I`, `↑↓`
   See DIRECTORIES — LOCATING FILES, page 25.
4. Select Open . . . . `↵`
   Convert File Format dialog box appears.
5. Select OK to confirm format and retrieve file . . . . . . `↵`

   OR   **OR**

   Open Convert File Format From `↓` . . . . `F4`

   a) Select a format . . . . `↑↓`, `F4`

   b) Select OK . . . . `↵`

6. Edit document.
7. Select File menu . . . . `Alt`+`F`
8. Select Save . . . . `S`
9. Open Format `↓` . . . . `Alt`+`F`, `F4`
10. Select WordPerfect 5.1 . . . . `↑↓`, `F4`
11. Select Save . . . . `↵`

CUT (MOVE) OR COPY DATA

Moves or copies selected text or graphics box within a document, into another document or into another Windows application. Any attributes, such as underline, are placed on the Clipboard and moved or copied with text if pasted into a WordPerfect document.

NOTE: *Also see APPEND TO CLIPBOARD on page 2 and DRAG AND DROP TEXT on page 39.*

1. Select text (page 218) and or graphics box (page 97).

2. Select **E**dit menu . . . . **Alt** + **E**

3. Select **C**opy to copy data . . . . **C**

   OR   **OR**

   Select Cu**t** to move data . . . . **T**

FROM DOCUMENT WINDOW OR APPLICATION TO RECEIVE DATA

4. Place insertion point where data will be inserted.

5. Select **E**dit menu . . . . **Alt** + **E**

6. Select **P**aste . . . . **P**

NOTE: *Selected data remains on Clipboard until replaced with another selection.*

CROSS-REFERENCE

Use this feature to automatically link references in a document to specified targets (places to look in a document), such as a page, a table, a figure, or a footnote. Creating cross-references involves two basic steps:

- *Mark references (pages 19 and 21) and targets (pages 20 and 21).*
- *Generate the cross-references (page 90).*

Mark Reference Only

A reference is a place in your document where numbers, generated by WordPerfect, direct reader to other items (targets) in the document.

1. Place insertion point where reference will be inserted.

2. Type introductory text for cross-reference . . . . **text**
   (i.e, "Bald Eagle see page")

3. Press **Spacebar** . . . . **Space**

4. Select **T**ools menu . . . . **Alt** + **T**

Continued ...

20

5. Select Mar<u>k</u> Text . . . . `K`

6. Select Cross-<u>R</u>eference . . . . `R`

7. Select ○<u>R</u>eference . . . . `Alt`+`E`

8. Open Tie Re<u>f</u>erence To `[      ⬍]` . . . . . `Alt`+`F`, `F4`
   <u>and</u> select desired reference type . . . . **letter**
   <u>P</u>age Number, Paragraph/<u>O</u>utline, <u>F</u>ootnote Number,
   <u>E</u>ndnote Number, Fi<u>g</u>ure, <u>T</u>able Box, Te<u>x</u>t Box,
   <u>U</u>ser Box, Eq<u>u</u>ation Box

9. Select Target <u>N</u>ame text box . . . . `Alt`+`N`

10. Type a target name . . . . **name**

   NOTE: Write down the target name because when you
   mark your targets (see below), you must match this
   target name exactly as typed.

11. Select **OK** . . . . `↵`

   A ? appears at reference point.

12. Repeat steps 1-11 for all references to mark.

Mark Target Only

*Marks a target to which a reference (see Mark Reference Only) is linked.
With this procedure, the reference number will not appear until you
generate the cross-references (page 90).*

1. Place insertion point immediately after the target.

   NOTE: If necessary, press **Alt** + **F3** (Reveal Codes) to insure
   insertion point is at the correct location.

2. Select <u>T</u>ools menu . . . . `Alt`+`T`

3. Select Mar<u>k</u> Text . . . . `K`

4. Select Cross-<u>R</u>eference . . . . `R`

5. Select ○<u>T</u>arget . . . . `Alt`+`T`

6. Select Target <u>N</u>ame text box . . . . `Alt`+`N`

7. Type a target name . . . . **name**

   NOTE: The target name must match reference name exactly
   (see Mark Reference Only above).

8. Select **OK** . . . . `↵`

9. Repeat steps 1-8 for all targets to mark.

CROSS-REFERENCE (continued)

Mark Both Reference and Target

Marks a target and a reference and inserts the reference number in one operation.

1. Place insertion point where reference will be inserted.

2. Type introductory text for cross-reference . . . . **text**
   (i.e, "Bald Eagle, see page")

3. Press **Spacebar** . . . . `Space`

4. Select **T**ools menu . . . . `Alt`+`T`

5. Select Mar**k** Text . . . . `K`

6. Select Cross-**R**eference . . . . `R`

7. Select ○**R**eference and Target . . . . `Alt`+`R`

8. Open Tie Re**f**erence To `⬚ ◆` . . . . `Alt`+`F`, `F4`
   and select desired reference type . . . . **letter**
   *P*age Number, Paragraph/*O*utline, *F*ootnote Number,
   *E*ndnote Number, Fi*g*ure, *T*able Box, Te*x*t Box,
   *U*ser Box, Equa*t*ion Box

9. Select Target **N**ame text box . . . . `Alt`+`N`

10. Type a target name . . . . **name**

11. Select **OK** . . . . `⏎`

    NOTE: The message "After you choose OK, place the insertion point immediately after the item you want to reference and press <Enter> to mark it as the 'target'" appears.

12. Select **OK** . . . . `⏎`

13. Place insertion point immediately after the target.

    NOTE: If necessary, press Alt + F3 (Reveal Codes) to insure insertion point is located after the target.

14. **Enter** . . . . `⏎`

    NOTE: WordPerfect inserts Reference and Target codes, and the reference number is displayed at the reference marker.

15. Repeat steps 1-14 for all references to mark.

CROSS-REFERENCE (continued)

Generate Cross-Reference
See GENERATE on page 90.

DATE

Insert Date

Inserts current date as text or as a code. When you insert a date code, the current date is displayed whenever the document is opened, retrieved or printed.

NOTE: *Date is determined by your computer clock. If the date is displayed incorrectly, refer to your DOS manual to set the date and time on your computer.*

1. Place insertion point where date will be inserted.
2. Select **T**ools menu .... `Alt`+`T`
3. Select **D**ate .... `D`
4. Select **T**ext .... `T`
   to insert current date as text.

   OR   **OR**

   Select **C**ode .... `C`
   to insert current date as a code.

Predefined Date Format

Sets format of date displayed when you insert a date into your document.

1. Select **T**ools menu .... `Alt`+`T`
2. Select **D**ate .... `D`
3. Select **F**ormat .... `F`
4. Open `Predefined Dates ▼` .... `Alt`+`P`, `F4`
   and select desired format .... `↕`, `Space`
5. Select **OK** .... `↵`

DATE (continued)

Custom Date/Time Format

Creates and sets a custom date/time format.

1. Select **T**ools menu .... **Alt** + **T**

2. Select **D**ate .... **D**

3. Select **F**ormat .... **F**

4. Select **E**dit Date Format text box .... **Alt** + **E**

5. If necessary, place insertion point or delete codes.

6. Open [Date Codes ▼] .... **Alt** + **D**, **F4**

   and select desired date code .... **⬆⁄₄**, **Space**

   AND/OR   **AND/OR**

   Open [Time Codes ▼] .... **Alt** + **T**, **F4**

   and select desired time code .... **⬆⁄₄**, **Space**

7. Repeat steps 4-6 for each code to add.

8. Select **OK** .... **⏎**

DELETE CODES

1. If necessary, press **Alt + F3** .... **Alt** + **F3**
   to turn Reveal Codes on.

2. Place highlight on code to delete.

3. Press **Delete** .... **Del**

24

DELETE TEXT

Delete next character
- Press **Delete** .... `Del`

Delete previous character
- Press **Backspace** .... `BkSp`

Delete word at insertion point
- Press **Ctrl + Backspace** .... `Ctrl` + `BkSp`

Delete part of word to right of insertion point
1. Press **Ctrl + Shift + Right Arrow** .... `Ctrl` + `Shift` + `→`
2. Press **Delete** .... `Del`

Delete part of word to left of insertion point
1. Press **Ctrl + Shift + Left Arrow** ..... `Ctrl` + `Shift` + `←`
2. Press **Delete** .... `Del`

Delete text to right of insertion point to end of line
- Press **Ctrl + End** .... `Ctrl` + `End`

Delete text from insertion point to end of page
1. Press **Alt + Shift + PgDn** .... `Alt` + `Shift` + `PgDn`
2. Press **Delete** .... `Del`

Delete selected text
1. Select text (page 218) to delete.
2. Press **Delete** .... `Del`

DIRECTORIES — LOCATING FILES

*Directories are named locations in which files are stored. A subdirectory is a directory stored inside another directory. When a file is not in the current directory, you must specify the **path** to the file as shown below.*

When you see . . . . **path**

To specify: *Examples:*

   the root directory on a drive, type . . . . **B:**

   the subdirectory on a drive, type . . . . **C:\wpwin\doc**

   the drive, directory
   and filename, type . . . . **C:\wpwin\doc\john.ltr**

When you see . . . . **filespec**

To specify: *Example:*

   only files with DOC filename extensions, type . . . . . . ***.DOC**

In this example, the wildcard character *, indicates any consecutive characters in the filename. For more information about wildcards, refer to your DOS documentation.

Specify Location of Files using <u>Directories List Box</u>

FROM OPEN, RETRIEVE, SAVE AS, OR SELECT DIALOG BOX

1. Double-click on desired directory name
   in <u>D</u>irectories list box.

   NOTE: *To change to a directory above current directory,
   double-click on [..] at top of list.*

2. Repeat step 1 until desired directory becomes current.

Files in specified directory appear in the F̲iles list box.

Specify Location of Files using <u>Filename Text Box</u>

FROM OPEN, RETRIEVE, SAVE AS, OR SELECT DIALOG BOX

1. Select <u>F</u>ilename text box . . . . **Alt** + **F**

2. Type path to file(s) . . . . **path**

   Example: *c:\wpc\doc*

   To limit display to specific file types:

   - Type a filename pattern . . . . **filespec**
     in F̲ilename text box.

     Example: **.LTR*

3. **Enter** . . . .

Files in specified directory appear in the F̲iles list box.

26

Specify Location of Files using <u>Quick List</u>

The Quick List contains descriptive names of defined drive and directory locations that you frequently use. Also see QUICK LIST on page 196.

FROM OPEN, RETRIEVE, SAVE AS, OR SELECT DIALOG BOX

1. Select ☐<u>Q</u>uick List . . . . **Alt**+**Q**

2. Select desired directory in Quick List box . **Alt**+**U**, **↕**

   NOTE: *From the Quick List, you can type the descriptive name and WordPerfect will move the highlight to the item automatically as you type it.*

3. **Enter** . . . . **↵**

Files in specified directory appear in the <u>F</u>iles list box.

Select a File in Files List Box

FROM OPEN, RETRIEVE, SAVE AS, OR SELECT DIALOG BOX

NOTE: *If necessary, click on up or down scroll arrow to show additional files.*

- Click on name of file to select in <u>F</u>iles list box.

   OR

   Select desired file in <u>F</u>iles list box . . . . . . **Alt**+**↓**, **↕**

   NOTE: *From the Files list box, you can type the filename and WordPerfect will move the highlight to the file automatically as you type it.*

To select a file and close dialog box in one step:

- Double-click on name of file in <u>F</u>iles list box.

View File from Dialog Box

FROM OPEN OR RETRIEVE DIALOG BOX

1. Select file in <u>F</u>iles list box (see above).

2. Select <u>V</u>iew . . . . **Alt**+**V**

A view window opens displaying contents of selected file.

DIRECTORIES — LOCATING FILES (continued)

Change Default Directory for Current Work Session

After you specify the location of files from a dialog box, you can set the directory to be the default directory for the current work session.

FROM OPEN, RETRIEVE, SAVE AS, OR SELECT DIALOG BOX

- Select ☐**C**hange Default Dir . . . . **Alt**+**C**

Delete, Copy, Rename, Move, and Find Files from Dialog Box

With these steps, you can manage your files while selecting files.

FROM OPEN OR RETRIEVE DIALOG BOX

1. If necessary, select a file in **F**iles list box (page 26).
2. Open [**Options ▼**] . . . . **Alt**+**T**, **F4**
   and select one option:

   - **D**elete . . . . **D**
     - Select **D**elete . . . . **↵**
   - **C**opy . . . . **C**
     - a) Type destination directory in **T**o text box . . . . **path**
     - b) Select **C**opy . . . . **↵**
   - **M**ove/Rename . . . . **M**
     - a) Type destination directory or
       filename in **T**o text box . . . . **path** or **filename**
     - b) Select **M**ove . . . . **↵**
   - **F**ind Files (*WP5.2*) . . . . **F**
     OR   **OR**
     Find (*WP5.1*) . . . . **F**

   > **NOTE:** *In version WP 5.1 a Find dialog box will appear from which you can choose the kind of search you want. From WP 5.2 the Find Files dialog box will appear. See pages 78-81 for options.*

DISPLAY PITCH

Adjusts the amount of space one character occupies on screen so characters and codes do not overlap.

NOTE: Display Pitch does not affect printed text, but affects the way WordPerfect displays your document.

Set Display Font Adjustment for Normal Mode

NOTE: Make sure Draft Mode option from View menu is not selected (page 38).

1. Select **L**ayout menu .... `Alt` + `L`

2. Select **D**ocument .... `D`

3. Select **D**isplay Pitch .... `D`

4. Select ○**A**uto for automatic adjustment .... `A`

   OR   **OR**

   Select ○**M**anual for custom adjustment .... `M`

   a) Select increment box .... `Tab`

   b) Type percentage of normal (5-250) .... **number**

5. Select **OK** .... `↵`

Set Display Font Adjustment for Draft Mode

NOTE: Make sure Draft Mode option from View menu is selected (page 38).

1. Select **L**ayout menu .... `Alt` + `L`

2. Select **D**ocument .... `D`

3. Select **D**isplay Pitch .... `D`

4. Select ○A**u**to for automatic adjustment .... `U`

   OR   **OR**

   Select ○Ma**n**ual for custom adjustment .... `N`

   a) Select increment box .... `Tab`

   b) Type value (.025 - .5 inches) .... **number**

5. Select **OK** .... `↵`

DISPLAY SETTINGS (Preferences)

Changes default display options.

1. Select File menu .... `Alt` + `F`
2. Select Preferences .... `E`
3. Select Display .... `D`

To set document window display options:

- Select or clear desired option(s) in
  Document Window group:

  ☐ Text in Windows System Colors .... `T`
  determines if text color is set by
  Windows Control Panel or by WordPerfect.

  ☐ Graphics in Black and White .... `G`
  determines whether graphics are
  displayed on screen as color images
  or as black and white images.

  ☐ Auto Redisplay in Draft Mode .... `A`
  determines how text is formatted on
  screen after editing changes are made
  using Draft Mode.

  ☐ Display Columns Side By Side .... `C`
  determines whether columns are displayed
  side by side or on separate pages.

  ☐ Display Merge Codes .... `M`

  ☐ Display Sculptured Dialog Boxes .... `S`
  determines whether dialog boxes are
  displayed as normal Windows dialog boxes
  with plain lines, or as "sculptured" dialog
  boxes with chiseled lines on a gray background.

Continued ...

30

To display or hide scroll bars:

- Select or clear ☐ Display **V**ertical Scroll Bar . . . . . 🔲**V**

  AND/OR   **AND/OR**

  Select or clear ☐ Display **H**orizontal Scroll Bar . . . . 🔲**H**

To specify a hard return character:

Displays specified character whenever you press Enter.

a) Select D**i**splay As text box . . . . 🔲**Alt** + 🔲**I**

b) Type a character . . . . **character**

   NOTE: *Character will appear on screen but will not be printed or displayed in Reveal Codes.*

To set reveal codes window size:

a) Select Reveal Codes **W**indow size
   increment box . . . . 🔲**Alt** + 🔲**W**

b) Type percentage of window (1-99) . . . . **number**

To set zoom default:

a) Select **Z**oom . . . . 🔲**Alt** + 🔲**Z**

b) Select desired zoom option . . . . **character**

   50%, **7**5%, **1**00%, 15**0**%, **2**00%, **T**o Page Width

   OR   **OR**

   Select **O**ther . . . . 🔲**O**

   1) Select increment box . . . . 🔲**Tab**

   2) Type desired percentage (50-400) . . . . . . **number**

c) Select **OK** . . . . 🔲⏎

4. Select **OK** . . . . 🔲⏎

Units of Measure
See UNITS OF MEASURE on page 273.

Reveal Codes Colors
See REVEAL CODES on page 207.

Draft Mode Colors
See Draft Mode Colors on page 38.

DOCUMENT COMPARE

Compare Document

Compares current document on screen with a document on disk and marks the differences between them.

1. Select **T**ools menu . . . . **Alt** + **T**
2. Select Doc**u**ment Compare . . . . **U**
3. Select **A**dd Markings . . . . **A**

   NOTE: *If current document has already been saved, the name of the current document will be displayed in the Add Markings dialog box.*

4. Type filename of document on disk . . . . **filename**

   OR   **OR**

   Open File to Compare ⊟ **F4**
   and select desired file (pages 25, 26).

5. Select **C**ompare . . . . **↵**

   NOTE: *Differences are marked on a phrase-by-phrase basis, not word by word.*

Document Compare — Difference Indicators

Added phrases — A pair of Redline codes [Redln On][Redln Off] is placed around each added phrase. For color monitors, added phrases appear in red.

Deleted Phrases — A pair of Strikeout codes [Stkout on][Stkout off] is placed around each deleted phrase. For color monitors, a line is drawn through the phrase.

Moved Phrases — "THE FOLLOWING TEXT WAS MOVED" is inserted before moved phrases, and "THE PRECEDING TEXT WAS MOVED" is inserted after phrases that were moved.

32

DOCUMENT COMPARE (continued)

Remove Document Compare Markings

Restores current document to its original status (before comparison without markings).

1. Select **T**ools menu . . . . **Alt** + **T**
2. Select Doc**u**ment Compare . . . . **U**
3. Select **R**emove Markings . . . . **R**
4. Select **OK** to remove all markings . . . . **⏎**

   OR   **OR**

   Select ☐Leave **R**edline Marks . . . . **R**
   to retain added marked phrases.

   • Select **OK** . . . . **⏎**

Remove Document Compare Markings Using Undo

Removes all Document Compare markings immediately after Document Compare is used.

1. Select **E**dit menu . . . . **Alt** + **E**
2. Select **U**ndo . . . . **U**

DOCUMENT SUMMARY

Attaches descriptive information such as a general overview, descriptive name, type, creation date, author, typist, subject, account, keywords, and abstract to a document.

Create Document Summary

1. Select **L**ayout menu . . . . **Alt** + **L**
2. Select **D**ocument . . . . **D**
3. Select **S**ummary . . . . **S**

Continued ...

DOCUMENT SUMMARY — Create (continued)

To extract field information from last document summary and current document text:

NOTE: *This option will:*
- *Retrieve A̲uthor and T̲ypist entries saved from last document summary into proper text boxes.*
- *Retrieve first 160 characters of text following the subject search text heading (such as RE:) from current document into S̲ubject text box.*
- *Retrieve first 400 characters of current document into A̲bstract text box.*

a) Select E̲xtract . . . . `Alt`+`E`

b) Select Y̲es . . . . `Y`

4. Select desired text box categories:

- Descriptive N̲ame . . . . `Alt`+`N`
  - Type description for document . . . . **name**

- Descriptive T̲ype . . . . `Alt`+`T`
  - Type category type for categorizing with File Manager . . . . **type**

- Creation D̲ate . . . . `Alt`+`D`
  - Type date in mm/dd/yy or mm-dd-yy format, followed by time and **a** or **p** for AM or PM . . . . **date time**

    Examples: *03/13/89 2:45p*
    03-13-89 2:42a

  NOTE: *Creation D̲ate is automatically filled in by WordPerfect, depending on system's date and time, and will remain the same unless changed.*

- Au̲thor . . . . `Alt`+`U`
  - Type name of author, address, etc., up to 60 characters . . . . **author**

- Ty̲pist . . . . `Alt`+`Y`
  - Type typist name, title, etc., up to 60 characters . . . . **typist**

Continued ...

34

DOCUMENT SUMMARY — Create (continued)

- **S**ubject . . . . **Alt**+**S**
  - Type document subject
    up to 160 characters . . . . **subject**
- A**c**count . . . . **Alt**+**C**
  - Type any identifying information . . . . **text**
- **K**eywords . . . . **Alt**+**K**
  - Type additional descriptive information
    and identifying keywords . . . . **text**
- **A**bstract . . . . **Alt**+**A**
  - Type brief summary of document
    up to 400 characters . . . . **summary**

    NOTE: Press Ctrl + Enter to insert a hard return in this
    text box.

5. Select **OK** . . . . **↵**

Delete Document Summary

Deletes the document summary associated with the current document.

1. Select **L**ayout menu . . . . **Alt**+**L**
2. Select **D**ocument . . . . **D**
3. Select **S**ummary . . . . **S**
4. Select De**l**ete . . . . **Alt**+**L**
5. Select **Y**es . . . . **Y**

Print Document Summary

1. Select **L**ayout menu . . . . **Alt**+**L**
2. Select **D**ocument . . . . **D**
3. Select **S**ummary . . . . **S**
4. Select **P**rint . . . . **Alt**+**P**

DOCUMENT SUMMARY — Print (continued)

Save Document Summary as a File

1. Select Layout menu . . . . **Alt** + **L**

2. Select Document . . . . **D**

3. Select Summary . . . . **S**

4. Select Save As . . . . **Alt** + **V**

5. Type a filename in Save As text box . . . . **filename**

6. Select Save . . . . **↵**

7. Select OK . . . . **↵**

DOCUMENT WINDOW

*In WordPerfect you can open up to nine document windows at a time.
When you first open a document its window is maximized.
In File Manager you can open various view (document) windows to
help you manager your files.*

Select (Switch To) Document Window or Icon

• Click anywhere on desired window or icon.

OR

1. Select Window menu . . . . **Alt** + **W**

2. Select number of document window or icon . . . . . **number**
   NOTE: When you select an icon, WordPerfect opens it.

Reduce (Minimize) Document Window to an Icon

• Click on window's minimize button . . . . **▼**

OR

1. Select document window (see above) to reduce.

2. Open window's Control menu . . . . **Alt** + **−**

3. Select Minimize . . . . **N**

36

DOCUMENT WINDOW (continued)

Enlarge (Maximize) Document Window

- Click on window's maximize button . . . . ▣

OR

1. Select document window (page 35) to maximize.
2. Open window's Control menu . . . . **Alt** + ▬
3. Select Ma**x**imize . . . . **X**

Restore a Maximized Document Window to its Previous Size

- Click on maximized window's restore button . . . . ▤

OR

1. Select document window (page 35) to restore.
2. Open window's Control menu . . . . **Alt** + ▬
3. Select **R**estore . . . . **R**

Change Size and Shape of Document Window

NOTE: Because a window cannot be sized if it is maximized, you must first restore it (see above) before executing these steps.

- Drag border or corner of window to obtain desired size.
  Mouse pointer becomes ⤢ ⇕ ⇔ when you point to a corner or border of a window.

OR

1. Select document window (page 35) to resize.
2. Open window's Control menu . . . . **Alt** + ▬
3. Select **S**ize . . . . **S**
4. Press any **arrow** key <u>once</u> in direction of border to size **↕**
5. Press **arrow** keys . . . . **↕**
   until desired size is obtained
6. **Enter** . . . . ↵
7. Repeat steps 2-6 for each border to size.

DOCUMENT WINDOW (continued)

Arrange Document Windows

- Drag window's title bar to desired location.

OR

1. Select **W**indow menu .... **Alt** + **W**

2. Select **C**ascade .... **C**
   to arrange windows so that they overlap each other,
   with the title bar for each window remaining visible

   OR   **OR**

   Select **T**ile .... **T**
   to arrange windows so that each window takes up a
   portion of the screen, without overlapping another window

Scroll Document Window with Mouse

Scroll to view text within boundaries of windows and dialog boxes.

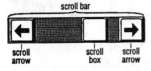

scroll bar

scroll arrow | scroll box | scroll arrow

Scroll to Any Position

- Drag scroll box in horizontal or vertical scroll bar to
  desired position.

Scroll Up or Down One Line

- Click on up or down scroll arrow.

Scroll Up or Down One Window

- Click on vertical scroll bar above or below the scroll box.

Scroll Left or Right One Window

- Click on horizontal scroll bar to left or right of the scroll box.

Close Document Window

See Close Document Window on page 11.

New Document Window

See NEW DOCUMENT WINDOW on page 161.

Open Document Window

See OPEN DOCUMENT WINDOW on page 167.

DRAFT MODE

Use draft mode to improve performance when editing text.

Set Draft Mode On/Off

1. Select View menu . . . . `Alt` + `V`
2. Select or deselect Draft Mode . . . . `D`

Draft Mode Colors

Determines what text will look like on screen when typing in Draft Mode.

NOTE: When typing in Draft Mode, differences in text attributes and text size are shown by color.

1. Select File menu . . . . `Alt` + `F`
2. Select Preferences . . . . `E`
3. Select Display . . . . `D`
4. Select Draft Mode Colors . . . . `Alt` + `D`
5. Open Predefined Display Colors `[    ⬦]` . `Alt` + `Y` , `F4`

   and select desired color setting . . . . **letter**

   Color, Monochrome, Blue On White, LCD Display,
   LCD Display - No Intensity, Plasma Display, Custom,

   If Custom was selected,

   a) Select desired item from Appearance,
      Sizes, or Other group . . . . `Alt` + **letter**

   b) Select desired color
      for item in Foreground
      Palette group . . . . `Alt` + `G` , `⇆` , `Space`

   c) Select desired color
      for item in Background
      Palette group . . . . `Alt` + `A` , `⇆` , `Space`

   d) Repeat step a-c for each attribute to set.

6. Select **OK** . . . . `↵`
7. Select **OK** . . . . `↵`

DRAG AND DROP TEXT

Move or copy selected text with a mouse.

Move Text

1. Drag through text to move.

   Also see SELECT TEXT on page 218.

2. Drag selection to desired location.

   Pointer becomes a ⌐⊡. *Vertical line indicates where text will be placed.*

Copy Text

1. Drag through text to copy.

   Also see SELECT TEXT on page 218.

2. Press and hold **Ctrl** . . . . `Ctrl`

   <u>and</u> drag selection to desired location.

   Pointer becomes a ⌐⊡. *Vertical line indicates where text will be placed.*

40

ENDNOTE

By default, WordPerfect places endnote text at the end of your document. To see your endnote text, you must print (page 184) or preview (page 188) your document. If you specify the placement of the endnotes (page 41), you must first generate (page 90) the endnote placement codes before printing.

Create Endnote

1. Place insertion point where endnote reference number will be inserted.
2. Select **L**ayout menu . . . . `Alt`+`L`
3. Select **E**ndnote . . . . `E`
4. Select **C**reate . . . . `C`
   The Endnote Window appears and displays number of endnote.
5. Type endnote . . . . **text**
6. Select **C**lose to save endnote
   and return to document . . . . `Alt`+`C`

WordPerfect inserts endnote number in docurnent and renumbers existing endnotes automatically.

Edit Endnote

1. Select **L**ayout menu . . . . `Alt`+`L`
2. Select **E**ndnote . . . . `E`
3. Select **E**dit . . . . `E`
4. Type number of endnote to edit . . . . **number**
5. Select **OK** . . . . `⏎`
6. Edit endnote.
7. Select desired option(s):

   - Note N**u**mber . . . . `Alt`+`U`
     to insert endnote number in endnote.

   - **P**revious Number . . . . `Alt`+`P`
     to edit previous endnote.

   - **N**ext Number . . . . `Alt`+`N`
     to edit next endnote.

8. Select **C**lose to save endnote . . . . `Alt`+`C`

ENDNOTE (continued)

Delete Endnote

• Delete [Endnote: #] code (see DELETE CODES on page 23).

NOTE: When you delete an endnote, WordPerfect automatically renumbers remaining endnotes.

Renumber Endnotes

Renumbers endnotes from insertion point forward.

1. Place insertion point where new numbering will begin.
2. Select **L**ayout menu . . . . **Alt**+**L**
3. Select **E**ndnote . . . . **E**
4. Select **N**ew Number . . . . **N**
5. Type new number . . . . **number**
6. Select OK . . . . **⏎**

Endnote Placement

Places endnotes text in a location other than at the end of a document.

1. Place insertion point where endnotes will be placed.
2. Select **L**ayout menu . . . . **Alt**+**L**
3. Select **E**ndnote . . . . **E**
4. Select **P**lacement . . . . **P**
5. Select **Y**es . . . . **Y**
   to place endnote text at insertion point and
   <u>restart endnote numbers</u> from this point forward.

   OR   **OR**

   Select **N**o . . . . **N**
   to place endnote text at insertion point and
   <u>continue with same endnote numbers</u>.

NOTE: WordPerfect inserts a comment (the comment will not print) that says: "It is not known how much space endnotes will occupy here. Generate to determine." The Comment box is followed by a hard page break.

Generate Endnote Placement

See GENERATE on page 90.

ENDNOTE OPTIONS

Changes made affect all endnotes in your document.

Continuous Endnotes

Sets the minimum number of inches an endnote will occupy before WordPerfect will split endnotes across a page.

1. Select **L**ayout menu . . . . **Alt**+**L**
2. Select **E**ndnote . . . . **E**
3. Select **O**ptions . . . . **O**
4. Select Minimum Note **H**eight text box . . . . **Alt**+**H**
5. Type height (inches) . . . . **number**
6. Select **OK** . . . . **↵**

Endnote Number Style and Appearance

Sets numbering style and appearance of endnotes from insertion point forward.

1. Select **L**ayout menu . . . . **Alt**+**L**
2. Select **E**ndnote . . . . **E**
3. Select **O**ptions . . . . **O**
4. Open N**u**mbering Method [＿＿▼] . . . . . **Alt**+**U**, **F4**
   and select desired numbering style:
   - **N**umbers — marks endnotes with numbers . . . . . . **N**
   - **L**etters — marks endnotes with letters . . . . **L**
   - **C**haracters — marks endnotes with characters . . . . **C**

   If Characters was selected,

   a) Select **C**haracters text box . . . . **Alt**+**C**
   b) Type desired character(s) to
      use for endnote numbering . . . . **character**

   NOTE: Character(s) is used once, then doubled, tripled, etc.

Continued ...

ENDNOTE OPTIONS (continued)

To edit endnote numbering style in <u>document text</u>:

a) Select Style in <u>T</u>ext text box . . . . [Alt]+[T]

b) If necessary, place insertion point and/or delete codes.

c) Open Style in <u>T</u>ext [◄] . . . . [F4]

   <u>an</u>d select desired text style . . . . **letter**

   Note Number, <u>B</u>old, <u>U</u>nderline, <u>D</u>ouble Underline,
   <u>I</u>talics, <u>O</u>utline, Shado<u>w</u>, S<u>m</u>all Caps, <u>R</u>edline,
   <u>S</u>trikeout, Sup<u>e</u>rscript, Subs<u>c</u>ript, <u>F</u>ine, <u>S</u>mall,
   <u>L</u>arge, <u>V</u>ery Large, E<u>x</u>tra Large

d) Repeat steps b and c as needed.

To edit endnote numbering style in <u>endnote text</u>:

a) Select Style in <u>N</u>ote text box . . . . [Alt]+[N]

b) If necessary, place insertion point and/or delete codes.

c) Open Style in <u>N</u>ote [◄] . . . . [F4]

   <u>an</u>d select desired text style . . . . **letter**

   Note Number, <u>B</u>old, <u>U</u>nderline, <u>D</u>ouble Underline,
   <u>I</u>talics, <u>O</u>utline, Shado<u>w</u>, S<u>m</u>all Caps, <u>R</u>edline,
   <u>S</u>trikeout, Sup<u>e</u>rscript, Subs<u>c</u>ript, <u>F</u>ine, <u>S</u>mall,
   <u>L</u>arge, <u>V</u>ery Large, E<u>x</u>tra Large

d) Repeat steps b and c as needed.

5. Select **OK** . . . . [↵]

44

Endnote Spacing

Sets line spacing within endnotes and spacing between endnotes from insertion point forward.

1. Select **L**ayout menu . . . . `Alt`+`L`
2. Select **E**ndnote . . . . `E`
3. Select **O**ptions . . . . `O`
4. Select **L**ine Spacing in Notes text box . . . . `Alt`+`L`
5. Type number (inches) . . . . **number**
6. Select Spacing **B**etween Notes text box . . . . `Alt`+`B`
7. Type number (inches) . . . . **number**
8. Select **OK** . . . . `↵`

ENVIRONMENT SETTINGS (Preferences)

1. Select **F**ile menu . . . . `Alt`+`F`
2. Select Pr**e**ferences . . . . `E`
3. Select **E**nvironment . . . . `E`

   To change <u>environment</u> settings:
   - Select or clear desired check boxes
     in Settings group . . . . **letter**

     *Auto Code **P**lacement, **C**onfirm on Code Deletion, Fast
     Sa**v**e, Allow **U**ndo, Allow **G**raphics Boxes to Bump to
     Next Page, **R**eformat Documents for Default Printer on Open*

   To change <u>beep</u> settings:
   - Select or clear desired check boxes
     in Beep On group . . . . **letter**

     *E**r**ror, **H**yphenation, **S**earch Failure*

   To change <u>menu</u> settings:
   - Select or clear desired check boxes
     in Menu group . . . . **letter**

     *Display Shortcut **K**eys, Display **L**ast Open Filenames*

Continued ...

ENVIRONMENT SETTINGS (continued)

To change <u>ruler</u> settings:

* Select or clear desired check boxes
  in Ruler group .... **letter**

*Tabs Snap to Ruler Grid, Show Ruler Guides, Ruler Buttons on
Top, Automatic Ruler Display*

To change <u>prompt for hyphenation</u> setting:

* Select desired radio button in
  Prompt for Hyphenation group .... **letter**

Never, When Required, Always External, Internal

To specify <u>location of hyphenation dictionary</u>:

* Select desired radio button in
  Hyphenation group .... **letter**

External, Internal

4. Select **OK** .... ⏎

FILE MANAGER

Organizes files on disks or network drives. Facilitates the renaming, copying, deleting, and moving of files.

Run File Manager from WordPerfect

1. Select File menu . . . . `Alt`+`F`
2. Select File Manager . . . . `F`

Run File Manager from Windows Program Manager

- Run WP File Manager . . . .

  Refer to your Windows documentation.

  WP
  File Manager

Open a File Manager View Window

File Manager has five types of windows; WP File Navigator, Viewer, File List, Quick List, and Search Results. A Search Results window will only appear when a search has been performed.

1. Select View menu from File Manager . . . . `Alt`+`V`
2. Select desired window to display:
   - File List . . . . `F`
   - WP File Navigator . . . . `N`
   - Viewer . . . . `V`
   - Quick List . . . . `Q`
3. To open additional windows repeat steps 1 and 2.

Select Preset Window Layout

1. Select View menu from File Manager . . . . `V`
2. Select Layouts . . . . `L`
3. Select desired preset layout . . . . `1/4`, `↵`
   - Wide Navigator, Viewer
   - Wide FileList, Viewer
   - Narrow FileList, Viewer
   - FileList, Viewer
   - QuickList, FileList, Viewer
   - Navigator, FileList, Viewer

FILE MANAGER (continued)

Add New Window Layout to Layouts Menu

1. Open desired view windows (page 46).

2. Size and arrange windows as desired.

3. Select <u>V</u>iew menu from File Manager . . . . `Alt` + `V`

4. Select <u>L</u>ayouts . . . . `L`

5. Select <u>S</u>etup . . . . `S`

6. Select Layout <u>N</u>ame text box . . . . `Alt` + `N`

7. Type name for new layout . . . . **name**

8. Select or clear ☐ Save <u>W</u>indow Contents
   with Layout . . . . `Alt` + `W`

   *NOTE: When checked, the same files and directories
   will appear when this layout is selected.*

9. Select <u>S</u>ave . . . . `Alt` + `S`

*File Manager adds the current arrangement of windows to the Layouts
menu. Up to ten layouts can be listed in the layout menu at one time.*

Delete Window Layout

1. Select <u>V</u>iew menu from File Manager . . . . `Alt` + `V`

2. Select <u>L</u>ayouts . . . . `L`

3. Select <u>S</u>etup . . . . `S`

4. Select layout to delete from List <u>o</u>f Layouts list box . . . `↑/↓`

5. Select <u>D</u>elete . . . . `Alt` + `D`

6. Select <u>Y</u>es to confirm deletion . . . . `↵`

7. Select **Close** . . . . `Alt` + `F4`

48

Change Startup Window Layout from View Menu

1. Open desired view windows (page 46).

   • Size and arrange windows as desired.

   OR

   Select a preset window layout (page 46).

2. Select <u>V</u>iew menu from File Manager . . . . `Alt`+`V`

3. Select <u>L</u>ayouts . . . . `L`

4. Select <u>S</u>etup . . . . `S`

5. Select {Startup} from List <u>o</u>f Layouts list box . . . . `↑`

6. Select or clear ☐Save <u>W</u>indow Contents
   with Layout . . . . `Alt`+`W`

   NOTE: *When checked, the same files and directories will
   appear when this layout is loaded.*

7. Select <u>S</u>ave . . . . `Alt`+`S`

8. Select <u>Y</u>es to overwrite previous layout {Startup} . . . . . `↵`

Change Startup Window Layout from Preferences

*The displayed layout when File Manager is closed, will become the new
Startup layout. This option takes precedence over selecting Startup
layout from View menu.*

1. Select <u>F</u>ile menu from File Manager . . . . `Alt`+`F`

2. Select Pr<u>e</u>ferences . . . . `E`

3. Select <u>E</u>nvironment . . . . `E`

4. Select ☐Save Current <u>L</u>ayout on Exit
   in Window/Layout Operations group . . . . `Alt`+`L`

5. Select **OK** . . . . `↵`

FILE MANAGER (continued)

Select Files and Directories

You can select files or directories (directory items) in a WP File Navigator, File List, Quick List, or Search Results window.

Select Files and Directories With Mouse

Select one directory item

- Click on desired file or directory.

Select multiple directory items in sequence

- Drag mouse through desired directory items.

OR

a) Click on first directory item.

b) Press **Shift** . . . . `Shift`
   <u>and</u> click on last directory item in group.

Select non-consecutive directory items

- Press and hold **Ctrl** . . . . `Ctrl`
  <u>and</u> click on each directory item.

AND/OR   **AND/OR**

- Press and hold **Ctrl** . . . . `Ctrl`
  <u>and</u> drag through directory items.

Deselect individual directory items

- Press and hold **Ctrl** . . . . `Ctrl`
  <u>and</u> click on each directory item.

Deselect all directory items

- Click on any directory item

Select Files and Directories Using Menu

Select or deselect all directory items in an active list

1. Select **E**dit menu from File Manager . . . . `Alt`+`E`

2. Select **S**elect All . . . . `S`

   OR   **OR**

   Select **U**nselect All . . . . `U`

FILE MANAGER (continued)

Select Files and Directories Using Keyboard

Selects files or directories in active list.

Select one directory item

- Press **Up** or **Down** arrow to select desired item . . . |↑/↓|

Select multiple directory items in sequence

1. Press **Up** or **Down** arrow to select first item . . . . . |↑/↓|

2. Press and hold **Shift** <u>and</u> press **Up**
   or **Down** arrow to expand selection . . . . . |Shift| + |↑/↓|

Select non-consecutive directory items

1. Press **Up** or **Down** arrow to select first item . . . . . |↑/↓|

2. Press **Shift + F8** (begin selection) . . . . . . |Shift| + |F8|

3. Press **Up** or **Down** arrow to move to next item . . . |↑/↓|

4. Press Space to select . . . . |Space|

5. Repeat steps 3 and 4 for each item to select or deselect.

6. Press **Shift + F8** (end selection) . . . . |Shift| + |F8|

Deselect directory items

- Press **Up** or **Down** arrow . . . . |↑/↓|

Open Files

If you opened File Manager from a WordPerfect application, this procedure will open a document file or files into separate document windows. If you are running File Manager as a separate application, Open will run a specified application and open the data file you have selected.

If File Manager was opened from WordPerfect,

1. Double-click on document file to open.

2. Click on . . . . **Open**

OR

1. Select document file(s) (pages 49, 50) to open.

2. Select <u>F</u>ile menu from File Manager . . . . |Alt| + |F|

3. Select <u>O</u>pen . . . . |O|

4. Select <u>O</u>pen . . . . |↵|

Continued ...

FILE MANAGER — Open Files (continued)

If File Manager was opened from Program Manager,

1. Double-click on data file to open.

   OR

   Select data file (pages 49,50) to open.

   a) Select File menu from File Manager . . . . `Alt`+`F`

   b) Select Open . . . . `O`

   If no association exists for data file,

   Select Application text box . . . . `Alt`+`A`

   • Type program filename in text box . . . . **filename**

     OR   **OR**

     Open Application ⊟ . . . . `F4`
     and select filename (pages 25,26)

2. Select Open . . . . `Alt`+`O`
   to open selected file into specified application.

Retrieve Files

If you opened File Manager from a WordPerfect application, this procedure will retrieve a file or files into one WordPerfect document window. If you are running File Manager as a separate application, Retrieve will run a specified application and open the data file you have selected.

If File Manager was opened from a WordPerfect,

FROM WORDPERFECT

1. Place insertion point where document(s) will be inserted.

FROM FILE MANAGER

2. Select document file(s) (page 49,50) to retrieve.

3. Select File menu from File Manager . . . . `Alt`+`F`

4. Select Retrieve . . . . `R`

5. Select Retrieve . . . . `↵`

Continued ...

52

If File Manager was opened from Program Manager,

1. Select data file(s) (page 49, 50) to open.
2. Select File menu from File Manager .... |Alt| + |F|
3. Select Retrieve .... |R|

   If no association exists for data file,

   Select Application text box .... |Alt| + |A|

   - Type program filename in text box .... **filename**

     OR   **OR**

     Open Application |⊟| .... |F4|
     and select filename (pages 25, 26).

4. Select Retrieve .... |↵|
   to open selected file(s) into specified application.

Create a New Directory

1. Select File menu from File Manager .... |Alt| + |F|
2. Select Create Directory .... |T|
3. Type full pathname of directory
   in New Directory text box .... **path**
   Example: c:\wpc\docs
4. Select Create .... |↵|

FILE MANAGER (continued)

Open WP File Navigator Window

Use the WP File Navigator to quickly move down the path of directories and subdirectories to locate files. From the WP File Navigator you can find, copy, delete, move, rename, view, open, print, and retrieve files, as well as change file attributes.

NOTE: *You can open more than one WP File Navigator window at a time.*

1. Select <u>V</u>iew menu from File Manager . . . . `Alt` + `V`

2. Select WP File <u>N</u>avigator . . . . `N`

NOTE: *The status bar at the bottom of File Manager displays information about currently selected drive or directory.*

Navigating in WP File Navigator:

WP Navigator Window Function:	Mouse Action:
Display contents of root directory of drive	Double-click on letter of drive in Drives list.
Display contents of directory	Double-click on desired directory name in list.
Display directory in a File List window	Click on title button of desired directory list.
Scroll through items in a list	Click on up or down scroll arrow of desired list.
Scroll to a list that is not in view	Click on direction button (>>) and (<<) at the left of WP File Navigator window until desired list is in view.

WP Navigator Window Function:	Keyboard Action:
Move to a Drives or directory list	Left, Right
Move to an item in active list	Up, Down
Display contents of root directory for selected drive in Drives list	Enter
Display contents of selected directory in a directory list	Enter
Move among lists and title buttons	Tab, Shift+Tab
Display directory in a File List window	Tab or Shift+Tab until desired title button is outlined, then press Enter.

FILE MANAGER (continued)

Open File List Window

The File List window displays contents of current directory and provides directory information such as filename, size, date and time of last revision, file attributes, full path, descriptive name and type. File List lets you find, copy, delete, move, rename, view, open, print, and retrieve files, as well as change file attributes.

NOTE: *You can open more than one File List window at a time.*

1. Select <u>V</u>iew menu from File Manager .... `Alt` + `V`
2. Select <u>F</u>ile List .... `F`

Change Directories in File List Window

• Double-click on name of directory in list to change to.

> ***NOTE:*** *Directory names are enclosed in square brackets [ ].
> To change to a directory above current directory,
> double-click on [..] at top of list.*

OR

Select <u>D</u>ir text box .... `Tab`

  a) Type full directory pathname .... **path**

> ***Example:*** *c:\wpdoc\letters*
> ***NOTE:*** *You can type a filespec to limit display of files in list.*

  b) **Enter** .... `↵`

Change Directory and Open a New File List Window

1. Select <u>F</u>ile menu from File Manager .... `Alt` + `F`
2. Select Change Directory .... `G`
3. Type full directory pathname in <u>D</u>irectory text box ... **path**
   OR   **OR**
   Select desired directory name
   in <u>D</u>irectories list box .... `Alt` + `I`, `↑↓`, `↵`
   OR   **OR**
   Select desired directory name
   in <u>Q</u>uick List list box .... `Alt` + `Q`, `↑↓`, `↵`
4. Select ☐ Open <u>N</u>ew File List .... `Alt` + `N`
5. Select **OK** .... `↵`

FILE MANAGER (continued)

Show Specific Files in a File List Window

1. Select or open a File List window (page 45).
2. Select **Dir** text box . . . . **Tab**
3. Type a filename pattern . . . . **filespec**
   *Example: *.LTR*
4. **Enter** . . . . **↵**

Add a Column in a File List or Search Results Window

1. Click on any blank space in heading bar where column will be added.
   NOTE: *You may need to maximize or size the File List or Search Results window.*
2. Click on desired column name from pop-up list.

Arrange Columns in a File List or Search Results Window

- Drag column heading to desired location on heading bar.

Resize Columns in a File List or Search Results Window

- Drag edge of column heading left or right.

Delete Columns in File List or Search Results Window

- Drag column heading off heading bar.

56

Change View Options In a File List Window

Changes order of files displayed in selected File List window.

1. Select or open a File List window (page 45).
2. Select **V**iew menu from File Manager . . . . `Alt`+`V`
3. Select **O**ptions . . . . `O`
4. Select **A**scending . . . . `Alt`+`A`

   OR   **OR**

   Select D**e**scending . . . . `Alt`+`E`
5. Select one option from Sort List By group:

   ○ Full **P**ath . . . . `Alt`+`P`

   ○ **F**ilename . . . . `Alt`+`F`

   ○ File E**x**tension . . . . `Alt`+`X`

   ○ File **S**ize . . . . `Alt`+`S`

   ○ **D**ate and Time . . . . `Alt`+`D`

   ○ Descriptive **N**ame . . . . `Alt`+`N`

   ○ Descriptive **T**ype . . . . `Alt`+`T`
6. Select or clear options from Display In List group:

   ☐ F**i**les . . . . `Alt`+`I`

   ☐ Di**r**ectories . . . . `Alt`+`R`

   ☐ **H**idden/System Files . . . . `Alt`+`H`
7. Select or clear ☐Doc Summary in **V**iewer . . . . . `Alt`+`V`
   to display Document Summary descriptive
   name and type when Viewer window is in use.
8. Select **OK** . . . . `↵`

FILE MANAGER (continued)

Open Quick List Window

The Quick List provides a way to name and access frequently used directories.

1. Select **V**iew menu from File Manager . . . . |Alt| + |V|

2. Select **Q**uick List . . . . |Q|

Add a Directory to Quick List

1. Select **V**iew menu from File Manager . . . . |Alt| + |V|

2. Select **E**dit Quick List . . . . |E|

   The Edit Quick List dialog box appears.

3. Select **A**dd . . . . |Alt| + |A|

4. Type a full directory path in **D**irectory/Filename box . . **path**

   OR   **OR**

   Open Directory/Filename |▣| . . . . |F4|
   an**d** select directory (page 25).

5. Select Descriptive **N**ame text box . . . . |Alt| + |N|

6. Type descriptive name . . . . **name**

7. Select **OK** to close dialog box . . . . |↵|

8. Select **OK** to return to File Manager . . . . |↵|

Use Quick List Window to Show Files in a File List Window

1. Select or open (see above) Quick List window.

2. Select (double-click on) desired directory name
   in Quick List window . . . . |↕|, |↵|

NOTE: *Contents of directory will appear in a File List window.*
If no File List window is open, File Manager will open one.

58

Edit or Delete a Quick List Directory Item

1. Select **V**iew menu from File Manager .... `Alt`+`V`
2. Select **E**dit Quick List .... `E`
3. Select desired item from **Q**uick List list box .... `↕`

   To delete a Quick List item:

   a) Select **D**elete .... `Alt`+`D`
   b) Select **Y**es to confirm deletion .... `↵`

   To edit a Quick List item:

   a) Select **E**dit .... `Alt`+`E`

      To change directory location:

      • Type new directory in **D**irectory/Filename
        text box .... **path**
        OR   **OR**
        Open **D**irectory/Filename File `▤` .... `F4`
        and select directory (page 26).

      To change description:

      1) Select Descriptive **N**ame .... `Alt`+`N`
      2) Type description for directory .... **text**

   b) Select **OK** .... `↵`

4. Select **OK** to return to File Manager .... `↵`

Open Viewer Window

Displays contents of file selected in a WP File Navigator, File List, or Search Results window. The Viewer window can display text, graphics, or codes. If a file contains both text and graphics, only text will be displayed. Refer to your documentation for information about supported graphic formats.

1. Select **V**iew menu from File Manager .... `Alt`+`V`
2. Select **V**iewer .... `V`

FILE MANAGER (continued)

Display Document Summary in Viewer Window

1. Select **V**iew menu from File Manager .... **Alt** + **V**
2. Select **O**ptions .... **O**
3. Select ☐Doc Summary in **V**iewer .... **Alt** + **V**
4. Select **OK** .... **↵**
5. From Viewer window, select [Summary]
   to view Document Summary .... **Tab**, **↵**

   • Select [Text] to see document again .... **↵**

Search Menu

The Search Menu provides the following options:

Find Words — locates files that contain specified words (page 60).

Find Files — locates files based on a supplied filespec (page 60).

Advanced Find — locates files containing specified words and/or files with a specified filespec (page 62).

Search Active Window — locates text fields as they appear in a Find Files or Search Results window or text in a Viewer window (page 61).

Word Search

In Find Words or Advanced Search, finds only alphanumeric characters and provides for the use of operators and wildcard characters as follows.

Finds files containing:	modifier:	example:
a phrase	""	"a phrase"
word with any character in ? position	?	word? (finds words, wordy)
word with any group of characters in * position	*	word* (finds Words**worth**)
both word1 and word2	space	word1 word2
either word1 or word2 or both words	,space	word1, word2
word1 but not word2	space-	word1 -word2

String Search

*In Find Words and Advanced Search, finds an exact **character-by-character** match of specified word or phrase. It will also find non alphabetic characters and extended characters.*

60

FILE MANAGER (continued)

Find Words

Searches files for specified word(s). You can search a WP File Navigator, File List, Quick List, or Search Results window, active window or selected files.

1. If desired, select files or directories (page 49) to search.
2. Select **S**earch menu from File Manager . . . . **Alt** + **S**
3. Select Find **W**ords . . . . **W**
4. Type word(s) to search for in **W**ord Pattern text box . . . **text**

   NOTE: See Word Search on page 59.

5. Select ○ **C**urrent Window . . . . **Alt** + **C**
   to search all files in active window

   OR   **OR**

   Select ○ **S**elected Item(s) . . . . **Alt** + **S**
   to search files selected in step 1.

6. Select **F**ind to begin search . . . . **⏎**

Search Results window appears showing files that contain words specified.

Find Files

Searches for files by filename or a filename pattern. You can search a WP File Navigator, File List, and Quick List, or Search Results window. Also see Find Files (see above) and QUICKFINDER (page 198).

1. Select directory or directories (pages 49, 50) to search.
2. Select **S**earch menu from File Manager . . . . **Alt** + **S**
3. Select Find **F**iles . . . . **F**
4. Type a filespec in **F**ile Pattern text box . . . . **filespec**

   *NOTE: Type a filename or use wildcard characters * and ?*
   to specify a filename pattern.
   *Example: *.BK!*

Continued ...

FILE MANAGER — Find Files (continued)

5. Select an option from Apply Find
   to Current group:

   ○ <u>S</u>elected Item(s) .... `Alt`+`S`

   ○ Su<u>b</u>tree .... `Alt`+`B`

   ○ <u>D</u>irectory .... `Alt`+`D`

   ○ D<u>r</u>ive .... `Alt`+`R`

6. Select <u>F</u>ind .... `↵`

Search Results window appears showing files you specified.

Search Active Window

In a File List or Search Results window, this procedure searches text fields (Filename, Descriptive Name, Descriptive Type, Full Pathname) as they appear in the window. In a Viewer window, this procedures searches the text of file shown in viewer.

1. Select or open File List window (page 54) to search.

   NOTE: *Make sure data to search is displayed in active File List window. See page 55 for Column options for these windows.*

   OR

   Select or Open a Viewer window (page 58) to search.

   OR

   Select a Search Results window.

   NOTE: *Make sure data to search is displayed in active Search Results window. See page 55 for Column options for these windows.*

2. Select <u>S</u>earch menu from File Manager .... `Alt`+`S`

3. Select <u>S</u>earch Active Window .... `S`

4. Type text to find .... **text**

   NOTE: *File Manager will search active window for text exactly as it is typed.*

Continued ...

FILE MANAGER — Search Active Window (continued)

5. Select ⭕Forward .... `Alt` + `F`

   OR   OR

   Select ⭕Backward .... `Alt` + `B`

6. Select Search .... `⏎`

File Manager selects first item containing search string in list.

Continue Search

Locates next or previous occurrence of string specified in a Search Active Window operation (previous page).

1. Select Search menu from File Manager .... `Alt` + `S`

2. Select Search Next .... `N`

   OR   OR

   Select Search Previous .... `P`

Advanced Find

Provides advanced search options that you can combine to quickly locate your files.

1. If necessary, select files or directories (page 49) to search.

2. Select Search menu from File Manager .... `Alt` + `S`

3. Select Advanced Find .... `A`

4. Type a filespec in File Pattern text box .... **filespec**

   NOTE: *Type a filename or use wildcard characters * and ? to specify a filename pattern.*
   Example: **.BK!*

   AND/OR   AND/OR

   Select Word Pattern text box .... `Alt` + `W`

   • Type word(s) or string to search for .... **text**

   NOTE: *See Word Search and String Search on page 59.*

5. Open Apply Find [◆] .... `Alt` + `A` , `F4`

   and select desired option .... **letter**

   Selected Item(s), Current Window, Current Directory, Current Subtree, Current Drive

   NOTE: *Your selections will determine available options.*

Continued ...

FILE MANAGER — Advanced Search (continued)

If a Word Pattern was entered in step 4,

- Open Find **M**ethod [⬦] . . . . `Alt`+`M`, `F4`
  <u>and</u> select desired option . . . . **letter**
  Word Search, String Search

  If Word Search was selected,

  - Open **L**imit Find To [⬦] . . . . `Alt`+`L`, `F4`
    <u>and</u> select desired option . . . . **letter**
    Document text, First Page, Document Summary,
    Descriptive Name, Descriptive Type, Author,
    Typist, Subject, Account, Key words, Abstracts

    AND   **AND**

    Open Find M**u**ltiple Words
    in Same [⬦] . . . . `Alt`+`U`, `F4`
    <u>and</u> select desired option . . . . **letter**
    File, Page, Section, Paragraph, Sentence, Line

To limit search to a date range:

a) Select **F**rom text box . . . . `Alt`+`R`

b) Type start date . . . . **mm/dd/yy**

c) Select **T**o text box . . . . `Alt`+`T`

d) Type ending date . . . . **mm/dd/yy**

6. Select or clear ☐**C**ase Sensitive . . . . `Alt`+`C`

   AND/OR   **And/OR**

   Select or clear ☐Word**P**erfect Files Only . . . . . . `Alt`+`P`

7. Select **F**ind . . . . `↵`

Search Results window appears showing files that match specified criteria.

64

Associate Files with an Application

*You can associate files with an application so that when you open,
retrieve, or print a file, File Manager opens the application it belongs to.*

Create or Change an Association by <u>File Type</u>

1. Select <u>F</u>ile menu from File Manager .... **Alt** + **F**
2. Select Pr<u>e</u>ferences .... **E**
3. Select <u>A</u>ssociate .... **A**
4. Open <u>F</u>ile Type ⬇ .... **Alt** + **F** , **F4**
5. Select file type to associate .... **↕** , **F4**
6. Select <u>A</u>ssociated Application
   text box in File Type Association group ...... **Alt** + **A**
7. Type filename of application .... **filename**

   NOTE: If necessary, type path to file (i.e., c:\windows\calc.exe).

   OR   **OR**

   Open <u>A</u>ssociated Application 🗁 **F4**
   <u>and</u> select filename (pages 25, 26).
8. Select <u>C</u>hange .... **Alt** + **C**
9. Select **Close** .... **Alt** + **F4**

Create or Change an Association by <u>File Extension</u>

1. Select <u>F</u>ile menu from File Manager .... **Alt** + **F**
2. Select Pr<u>e</u>ferences .... **E**
3. Select <u>A</u>ssociate .... **A**
4. Select File <u>E</u>xtension list box .... **Alt** + **E**
5. Type filename extension to associate .... **extension**

   OR   **OR**

   Select filename extension from list .... **↕**
6. Select <u>A</u>ssociated Application
   text box in File Extension Association group .... **Alt** + **S**

Continued ...

FILE MANAGER — Create or Change an Association File Extension (continued)

7. Type filename of application . . . . **filename**

   NOTE: *If necessary, type path to file (i.e., c:\windows\calc.exe).*

   OR

   Open A<u>s</u>sociated Application ⊟ **F4**
   <u>an</u>d select filename (pages 25, 26).

8. Select C<u>h</u>ange . . . . **Alt**+**H**

   OR   **OR**

   Select A<u>d</u>d if a new file extension
   was typed in step 5 . . . . **Alt**+**D**

9. Select **Close** . . . . **Alt**+**F4**

Delete a File Extension Association

1. Select <u>F</u>ile menu from File Manager . . . . **Alt**+**F**

2. Select Pr<u>e</u>ferences . . . . **E**

3. Select <u>A</u>ssociate . . . . **A**

4. Select extension to remove
   in File E<u>x</u>tension list box . . . . **Alt**+**E**, **↕**

5. Select De<u>l</u>ete . . . . **Alt**+**L**

6. Select **Close** . . . . **Alt**+**F4**

Start Application using Run Command

1. Select <u>F</u>ile menu from File Manager . . . . **Alt**+**F**

2. Select R<u>u</u>n . . . . **U**

3. Type filename of application to run
   in <u>F</u>ilename text box . . . . **filename**

   NOTE: *If necessary, type path to file (i.e., c:\windows\calc.exe).*

   OR   **OR**

   Open <u>F</u>ilename ⊟ **F4**
   <u>an</u>d select filename (pages 25, 26).

4. Select <u>R</u>un . . . . **↵**

66

FILE MANAGER (continued)

Start Application from Application Menu

1. Select **A**pplications menu from File Manager ... `Alt`+`A`
2. Select application name to run .... `⇅`, `↵`

Add Application to Application Menu

1. Select **A**pplications menu from File Manager ... `Alt`+`A`
2. Select **A**ssign to Menu .... `A`
3. Select Descriptive **N**ame text box .... `Alt`+`N`
4. Type description for application .... **name**
5. Select Command **L**ine text box .... `Alt`+`L`
6. Type filename of application .... **filename**

   NOTE: If necessary, type path to file (i.e., c:\windows\calc.exe).

7. If desired, select

   ☐Send Selected **F**iles to this Application ..... `Alt`+`F`

   *NOTE: If checked, selected files will open into the application
   you start from the Applications menu (see above).*

8. Select **A**dd .... `Alt`+`A`
9. Select **OK** .... `Tab`, `↵`

Delete Application from Application Menu

*NOTE: This procedure will not delete the application file
from disk.*

1. Select **A**pplications menu from File Manager ... `Alt`+`A`
2. Select **A**ssign to Menu .... `A`
3. Select application to delete from the
   List **o**f Applications list box .... `⇅`
4. Select **D**elete .... `Alt`+`D`
5. Select **Y**es .... `Y`
6. Select **OK** .... `Tab`, `↵`

   *Press **Tab** until OK is outlined.*

FILE MANAGER (continued)

Change Application on Application Menu

1. Select Applications menu from File Manager ... `Alt`+`A`

2. Select Assign to Menu .... `A`

3. Select application to change in
   List of Applications list box .... `↑↓`

4. If desired, select Descriptive Name text box .... `Alt`+`N`

   • Type new descriptive name .... **name**

5. If desired, select Command Line text box ...... `Alt`+`L`

   • Type new filename. .... **filename**
     NOTE: If necessary, type path to file (i.e., c:\windows\calc.exe).
     OR   **OR**
     Open Command Line ⊟ .... `F4`
     and select filename (pages 25, 26).

6. If desired, select or clear
   ☐Send Selected Files to this Application ...... `Alt`+`F`
   *NOTE: If checked, selected files will open into the application
   you start from the Applications menu (page 66).*

7. Select Change .... `Alt`+`C`

8. Select OK .... `Tab`, `↵`
   Press Tab until OK is outlined.

Change Display Font
Changes the font and point size of text displayed in File Manager.

1. Select View menu from File Manager .... `Alt`+`V`

2. Select Font .... `T`

3. Select desired font in Font list box .... `↑↓`

4. Select Size list box .... `Alt`+`S`

5. Select point size .... `↑↓`
   OR   **OR**
   Type a font size if selected font is scalable ..... **number**
   Preview window displays font appearance.

Continued ...

68

6. Select or clear ☐**B**old .... `Alt`+`B`
7. Select or clear ☐**I**talic .... `Alt`+`I`
8. Open **A**pply Font To 🔽 .... `Alt`+`A`, `F4`
   and select window(s) to apply
   font change to .... `↑⁄₄`, `F4`
9. Select **OK** .... `↵`

Copy a Single File or Directory

You can copy a file or directory from File List, WP File Navigator, Search Results, or Quick List windows. Also see Copy Files or Directories with Mouse on page 74.

1. If desired, select file or directory (pages 49, 50) to copy.
2. Select **F**ile menu from File Manager .... `Alt`+`F`
3. Select **C**opy .... `C`

   If a file or directory was not selected in step 1,

   a) Select **F**ile(s) to Copy text box .... `Alt`+`I`
   b) Type a filename .... **filename**
      NOTE: If necessary, type path to file (i.e., c:\doc\letter.frm).
      OR   **OR**
      Type directory name .... **path**
      Example: c:\wpdoc
4. Select **T**o text box .... `Alt`+`T`
5. Type destination directory
   and/or filename .... **path** and/or **filename**
   Examples: B:\DATA
                  B:\DATA\NewName
                  NewName
   OR   **OR**
   Open **T**o 🔽 .... `F4`
   and select destination drive and directory (pages 25, 26).

Continued ...

FILE MANAGER — Copy a Single File or Directory (continued)

6. If desired, clear
   ☐ Replace <u>F</u>iles with Same Name . . . . **Alt** + **F**

7. If desired, clear ☐ Confirm <u>R</u>eplace . . . . **Alt** + **R**

8. Select <u>C</u>opy . . . . **↵**

   If copying a directory,

   a) If directory specified in step 5 does not exist,
      select **OK** to create directory . . . . **↵**

   b) Select one option:

      • <u>F</u>iles in Directory Only . . . . **Alt** + **F**

      • Files in <u>D</u>irectory and Subdirectories
        — Copy to a Single Directory . . . . **Alt** + **D**

      • Files in Directory and <u>S</u>ubdirectories
        — Maintain Directory Structure . . . . **Alt** + **S**

   c) Select **OK** to begin copy . . . . **↵**

Copy Multiple Files or Directories

You can copy files or directories from File List, WP File Navigator, Search Results, or Quick List windows. Also see Copy Files or Directories with Mouse on page 74.

1. Select files or directories (pages 49, 50) to copy.

2. Select <u>F</u>ile menu from File Manager . . . . **Alt** + **F**

3. Select <u>C</u>opy . . . . **C**

4. If desired, clear
   ☐ Replace <u>F</u>iles with Same Name . . . . **Alt** + **F**

5. If desired, clear ☐ Confirm <u>R</u>eplace . . . . **Alt** + **R**

   If copying all items to <u>one directory</u>,

   a) Select <u>T</u>o Directory text box . . . . **Alt** + **T**

   b) Type destination drive and directory . . . . **path**

      OR   **OR**

      Open <u>T</u>o Directory ▤ **F4**
      <u>and</u> select drive and directory (pages 25, 26).

Continued ...

70

c) Select Copy **A**ll . . . . `Alt`+`A`

d) If directory specified in step b does not exist,
select **Y**es to create directory . . . . `↵`

If copying directories,

1) Select one option:

- **F**iles in Directory Only . . . . `Alt`+`F`

- Files in **D**irectory and Subdirectories
— Copy to a Single Directory . . . . . . `Alt`+`D`

- Files in Directory and **S**ubdirectories
— Maintain Directory Structure . . . . . `Alt`+`S`

2) If desired, select
☐**A**pply to All Selected Directories . . . . . `Alt`+`A`

3) Select **OK** . . . . `↵`

If copying items to <u>different directories</u>:

a) Select **T**o Directory text box . . . . `Alt`+`T`

b) Type destination directory . . . . **path**
for selected item in **F**iles to Copy list box.

OR   **OR**

Open **T**o Directory ⊟ . . . . `F4`
and select directory (pages 25, 26).

c) Select **C**opy . . . . `Alt`+`C`

d) If directory specified in step a does not exist,
select **OK** to create directory . . . . `↵`

If copying directories,

1) Select one option:

- **F**iles in Directory Only . . . . `Alt`+`F`

- Files in **D**irectory and Subdirectories
— Copy to a Single Directory . . . . . . `Alt`+`D`

- Files in Directory and **S**ubdirectories
— Maintain Directory Structure . . . . . `Alt`+`S`

Continued ...

FILE MANAGER — Copy Multiple Files or Directories (continued)

   2) Select or clear
      ☐Apply to All Selected Directories . . . . . **Alt** + **A**

   3) Select **OK** . . . . **⏎**

   e) Repeat steps a-d for each item to copy.

Move/Rename Single File or Directory

You can move and rename a file or directory selected in a File List, WP File Navigator, Quick List, or Search Results window. Also see Move Files or Directories with Mouse on page 75.

1. Select file or directory (pages 49, 50) to move or rename.

2. Select **File** menu from File Manager . . . . **Alt** + **F**

3. Select **Move/Rename** . . . . **M**

   If moving an item:

   • Type destination directory in **To** text box . . . . **path**
   OR   **OR**
   Open **To** **⊟** **F4**
   and select directory (pages 25, 26).

   If renaming an item in current directory:

   • Type new name in **To** text box . . . . **filename**

   If moving and renaming an item:

   • Type destination directory and
     new name in **To** text box . . . . **path\filename**

4. If desired, clear
   ☐Replace **Files** with Same Name . . . . **Alt** + **F**

5. If desired, clear ☐Confirm **Replace** . . . . **Alt** + **R**

6. Select **Move** . . . . **⏎**

7. If directory specified does not exist,
   select **OK** to create directory . . . . **⏎**

72

Move/Rename Multiple Files or Directories

You can move and rename files or directories selected in a File List, WP File Navigator, Quick List, or Search Results window. Also see Move Files or Directories with Mouse on page 75.

1. Select files or directories (pages 49, 50) to move or rename.

2. Select File menu from File Manager .... Alt + F

3. Select Move/Rename .... M

4. If desired, clear
   ☐Replace Files with Same Name .... Alt + F

5. If desired, clear ☐ Confirm Replace .... Alt + R

   If moving all items to one directory:

   a) If necessary, select To Directory text box ... Alt + T

   b) Type destination directory .... **path**

   OR   **OR**

   Open To ⊟ F4
   and select directory (pages 25, 26).

   c) Select Move All .... ↵

   d) If directory specified in step b does not exist,
      select OK to create directory .... ↵

   If moving each item to a different directory:

   a) If necessary, select To Directory text box ... Alt + T

   b) Type destination directory .... **path**
      for item selected in Files to Move list.

   OR   **OR**

   Open To ⊟ F4
   and select directory (pages 25, 26).

   c) Select Move .... Alt + M

   d) If directory specified in step b does not exist,
      select OK to create directory .... ↵

Continued ...

FILE MANAGER — Move/Rename Multiple Files or Directories
(continued)

e) Repeat steps a-d for each selected item in
Files to Move list box.

If <u>renaming all files</u> in one step:

a) If necessary, select To Directory text box ... `Alt`+`T`

b) Type a filespec .... **filespec**

   Example: *.doc to give all selected files a DOC
               filename extension.

c) Select Move All .... `↵`

74

Copy or Move Files and Directories with Mouse

With the mouse, you can copy or move files or directories between any WP File Navigator or File List window. You can also copy or move items from a Quick List or Search Result window to any WP File Navigator or File List window.

NOTE: *If the destination window is a <u>WP File Navigator window</u>, items will be moved or copied to the directory that appears in the destination <u>column heading</u>.*

If the destination window is a <u>File List window</u>, items will be moved or copied to the directory that appears in the window's title bar.

<u>Copy</u> Files or Directories with Mouse

1. Arrange source and destination windows so that both are in view.

   OR

   Select desired View layout (page 46).

   If copying items to another directory on <u>same drive</u>:

   • Press **Ctrl** . . . . [Ctrl]
     <u>and</u> drag through consecutive items to copy,
     <u>and without releasing mouse button,</u>
     drag items onto list in destination window.

   If copying items to a <u>different drive</u>,

   • Drag through consecutive items to copy,
     <u>and without releasing mouse button,</u>
     drag items onto list in destination window.

2. If desired, click on . . . □Replace **F**iles with Same Name
   to clear it.

3. If desired, click on . . . . □Confirm **R**eplace
   to clear it.

4. Click on . . . . **C**opy

Move Files or Directories with Mouse

1. Arrange source and destination windows so that both are in view.

   OR

   Select desired View layout (page 46).

   If moving items to a directory on <u>same drive</u>,

   • Drag through consecutive items to move,
   <u>and without releasing mouse button</u>,
   drag items onto list in destination window.

   If moving items to a <u>different drive</u>,

   • Press and hold **Alt** . . . . `Alt`
   <u>and</u> drag through consecutive items to copy,
   <u>and without releasing mouse button</u>,
   drag items onto list in destination window.

2. If desired, click on . . . ☐ **Replace Files with Same Name** to clear it.

3. If desired, click on . . . . ☐ **Confirm Replace** to clear it.

4. Click on . . . . **Move**

FILE MANAGER (continued)

Delete Files and Directories

1. Select files or directories (pages 49, 50) to delete.

2. Press **Delete** .... `Del`

   OR   **OR**

   Select **F**ile menu from File Manager .... `Alt`+`F`

   - Select **D**elete .... `D`

   If deleting a <u>single file</u>:

   - Select **D**elete .... `⏎`

   If deleting a <u>single directory</u>:

   a) Select **D**elete .... `⏎`

   b) Select one option:

   - **F**iles in Directory Only .... `Alt`+`F`

   - Files in **D**irectory and Subdirectories .... `Alt`+`D`

   - Files in Directory and **S**ubdirectories
     — Delete Directory Structure .... `Alt`+`S`

   c) Select **OK** .... `⏎`

   If deleting <u>multiple files or directories</u>:

   - Select Delete **A**ll .... `⏎`

     If deleting directories,

     NOTE: *When "Delete contents of directory .." message*
     *appears, Select **Y**es only if it's ok to delete files*
     the directory contains.

   a) Select one option:

   - **F**iles in Directory Only .... `Alt`+`F`

   - Files in **D**irectory and Subdirectories . `Alt`+`D`

   - Files in Directory and **S**ubdirectories
     — Delete Directory Structure .... `Alt`+`S`

   b) If desired, select
      ☐**A**pply to All Selected Directories ..... `Alt`+`A`

   c) Select **OK** .... `⏎`

FILE MANAGER (continued)

Print WordPerfect Document Files from File Manager

1. Select WordPerfect documents (pages 49, 50) to print.
2. Select File menu from File Manager . . . . `Alt`+`F`
3. Select Print . . . . `P`
4. Select Print . . . . `↵`

Print Other Data Files from File Manager

NOTE: *These steps require that you start File Manager from Window's Program Manager (page 46).*

1. Select data file (pages 49, 50) to print.
2. Select File menu from File Manager . . . . `Alt`+`F`
3. Select Print . . . . `P`

   If selected data file does not belong to application displayed in Application text box,

   - Type application filename
     in Application text box . . . . **path\filename**
     NOTE: *If necessary, type path to file (i.e., c:\windows\notepad.exe)*

   OR   **OR**

   Open Application `⊟` . . . . `F4`
   and select filename (pages 25, 26).

   If format in File Type list box is "unknown" or does not belong to application,

   a) Open File Type `⬛` . . . . `Alt`+`T`, `F4`
   b) Select desired format type . . . . `↕`, `F4`

4. Select Print . . . . `↵`

78

Print Directory Information

Prints information about files and directories as displayed in active window.

1. Select window containing information to print.

2. If desired, select items in window (pages 49, 50) to print.

3. Select **F**ile menu from File Manager . . . . **Alt** + **F**

4. Select Print **W**indow . . . . **W**

5. Select desired option . . . . **letter**

   Print List of Selected Files, Print Entire List, Print All Quick List Items

   NOTE: *Options depend on window selected.*

6. Select **OK** . . . . **⏎**

Close File Manager View Windows

See Close Document Windows on page 11.

Close File Manager

See Close (Exit) WordPerfect or File Manager on page 11.

FIND FILES *WP5.2*

Locates files that contain specified words and/or a specified filename or filename pattern. You can search directories, subdirectories (subtrees), and disk as well as the results of previous searches. You can also use QuickFinder indexes (page 198) to dramatically improve search time.

1. Select **F**ile menu . . . . **Alt** + **F**

2. Select Fin**d** Files . . . . **D**

   To change search directory:

   Default search directory is displayed at bottom of dialog box.

   • Type directory to search in File **P**attern text box . . **path**

   OR   **OR**

   Open File **P**attern ▣ **F4**

   and select directory (pages 25, 26).

   To limit search to a specific filename pattern:

   • Type a filespec in File **P**attern text box . . . . . . **filespec**

   Example: *.DOC

   Continued ...

FIND FILES (continued)

To limit search to files that contains specified words or phrases:

a) Select <u>W</u>ord(s) text box . . . . `Alt` + `W`

b) Type word(s) or phrase to search for . . . . **text**

> **NOTE:** *You can use the following modifiers between words, if not searching for a phrase:*

<u>Search and finds files containing</u>:	<u>modifier</u>:	<u>example</u>:
specified phrase	""	"a phrase"
word with any character in ? position	?	word? (finds words, wordy)
word with any group of characters in * position	*	word* (finds Wordsworth)
both word1 and word2	space	word1 word2
either word1 or word2 or both words	,space	word1, word2
word1 but not word2	space-	word1 -word2
both words that are a specified distance from each other	space /n	word1 word2 /25
both words, when words are on same line	space /lin	word1 word2 /lin
both words, when words are in same sentence	space /sen	word1 word2 /sen
both words, when words are in same paragraph	space /par	word1 word2 /par
both words, when words are on same page	space /pag	word1 word2 /pag
both words, when words are between sections (hard pages)	space /sec	word1 word2 /sec

If searching for a phrase,

- Select ☐Words Must Be <u>N</u>ext to Each Other . . . . `Alt` + `N`

Continued ...

80

To extend search to files other than Word Perfect documents:

- Clear ☐W__o__rdPerfect Documents Only . `Alt`+`O`

To specify where to search:

- Select one option in Search group:

  ○ D__i__rectory .... `Alt`+`R`

  ○ __S__ubtree .... `Alt`+`S`

  ○ __D__isk .... `Alt`+`D`

  ○ Search Results __L__ist .... `Alt`+`L`

    NOTE: This option is available only after a previous search.

  ○ __Q__uickFinder Index: .... `Alt`+`Q`

    NOTE: This option is available only if a QuickFinder index (page 198) exists. You cannot search a QuickFinder index for a filename pattern.

    1) Open QuickFinder Index ⬇ .... `⬇`

    2) Select index name to search .... `↹`, `F4`

3. Select __F__ind .... `↵`

FROM SEARCH RESULTS DIALOG BOX

To open a file:

a) Select file to open in __S__earch Results list box ..... `↹`

b) Select __O__pen .... `Alt`+`O`

To view contents of a file:

a) Select file to view in __S__earch Results list box ..... `↹`

b) Select __V__iew .... `Alt`+`V`

Continued ...

FIND FILES (continued)

To search View window for other words:

a) Open view window (previous page).

b) Select View window . . . . `Alt`+`Shift`+`F6`

c) Press **F2** (Search) . . . . `F2`

d) Type word(s) to search for in Fi<u>n</u>d text box . . . . . . **text**

e) To find word within other words,
   deselect ☐Match <u>W</u>hole Word Only . . . . `Alt`+`W`

f) Select <u>B</u>ackward . . . . `Alt`+`B`

   OR   **OR**

   Select <u>F</u>orward . . . . `Alt`+`F`

g) Select <u>S</u>earch . . . . `⏎`

h) Repeat steps c-g as needed.

i) Close View window . . . . `Alt`+`F4`

To perform a new search:

a) Select <u>F</u>ind Files . . . . `Alt`+`F`

b) Select desired options (see steps above).

To delete, copy, move, or rename files:

a) Select file to change . . . . `↕`

b) Open `Options ▼` . . . . `Alt`+`T`, `F4`

   <u>and</u> select desired option (page 27) . . . . **letter**

4. Select **Cancel** . . . . `Alt`+`F4`
   to close Search Results dialog box.

FLUSH RIGHT

Aligns text with the right margin. Also see JUSTIFICATION on page 135.

Flush Right Text

Aligns an existing line of text, or one line of text as it is typed, with right margin.

1. Place insertion point where alignment will begin.
2. Select <u>L</u>ayout menu . . . . `Alt`+`L`
3. Select <u>L</u>ine . . . . `L`
4. Select <u>F</u>lush Right . . . . `F`
5. If desired, type text . . . . **text**

Flush Right with Dot Leaders

Aligns an existing line of text, or one line of text as it is typed, with right margin and inserts dot leaders.

1. Place insertion point where alignment will begin.
2. Select <u>L</u>ayout menu . . . . `Alt`+`L`
3. Select <u>L</u>ine . . . . `L`
4. Select <u>F</u>lush Right . . . . `F`
5. Repeat steps 2-4 to add dot leader.
6. If desired, type text . . . . **text**

FONT

Changes the appearance (such as *italic*), *size* (such as 14 pt), *and typeface* (such as courier) *of the text in a printed document. You can make changes to fonts in three dialog boxes: Printer Initial Font, Document Initial Font, and Font.*

NOTE: *Fonts displayed in the F**o**nts list box are those currently installed for selected printer.*

Printer Initial Font

Sets initial font for all documents created for selected printer. The font is in effect unless changes are made to fonts with Document Initial Font or Font dialog boxes.

1. Select File menu .... **Alt** + **F**

2. Select Select Printer .... **L**

3. Select desired printer from Available
   Printers list box .... **↑↓**

4. Select Setup .... **Alt** + **E**

5. Select Initial Font .... **Alt** + **F**

6. Select desired font in Fonts list box .... **↑↓**

   If font is scalable,

   a) Select Point Size text box .... **Alt** + **Z**

   b) Type point size .... **number**

      OR   **OR**

      Select desired point size .... **↑↓**

7. Select OK .... **↵**

8. Select OK .... **↵**

9. Select Select .... **↵**

Document Initial Font

Sets the font for the current document. The font will remain in effect until another font code is encountered. Document Initial Font overrides font selection made in Printer Initial Font dialog box.

1. Select Layout menu .... **Alt** + **L**

2. Select Document .... **D**

Continued ...

FONT — Document Initial Font (continued)

3. Select Initial **F**ont . . . . ▢**F**
4. Select desired font in F**o**nts list box . . . . ▢
   If font is scalable,
   a) Select Point Si**z**e text box . . . . ▢**Alt**+▢**Z**
   b) Type point size . . . . **number**
      OR   **OR**
      Select desired point size . . . . ▢
5. Select **OK** . . . . ▢

Change Base Font

Changes font from insertion point forward, or until another font code is encountered. This code overrides font selections made in both Printer Initial Font and Document Initial Font dialog boxes.

1. Place insertion point where font change will begin.
2. Select F**o**nt menu . . . . ▢**Alt**+▢**O**
3. Select F**o**nt . . . . ▢**O**
4. Select desired font in F**o**nt list box . . . . ▢
   If font is scalable,
   a) Select Point Si**z**e text box . . . . ▢**Alt**+▢**Z**
   b) Type point size . . . . **number**
      OR   **OR**
      Select desired point size . . . . ▢
5. Select **OK** . . . . ▢

FONT ATTRIBUTES

Changes the appearance (such as **BOLD** or *Italics*) *or size of text* (such as Small or Large) *in document.*

Font Appearance/Size

1. Select text (page 218) to apply font attributes to.

   OR

   Place insertion point where font attributes will begin.

2. Select Font menu . . . . `Alt` + `O`

3. Select Font . . . . `O`

4. Select or clear desired appearance attribute(s)
   from Appearance group . . . . `Alt` + letter

   *Bold, Underline, Double Underline, Italic,
   Outline, Shadow, Small Cap, Redline, Strikeout*

   AND/OR   **AND/OR**

   Select or clear desired size attribute(s)
   from Size group . . . . `Alt` + letter

   *Superscript, Subscript, Fine, Small, Large,
   Very Large, Extra Large*

5. Select OK . . . . `⏎`

   If text was selected,

   • Press **Right** arrow to deselect text . . . . `→`

   If text was not selected,

   a) Type text . . . . **text**

   b) Repeat steps 2-5 to change font appearance or size.

Return Font to Normal

1. Select text (page 218) to make normal.

   OR

   Place insertion point where normal text will begin.

2. Select Font menu . . . . `Alt` + `O`

3. Select Normal . . . . `N`

FOOTNOTE

WordPerfect places footnote text at bottom of page where they are referenced. To see your footnote text, you must print (page 184) or preview (page 188) your document.

Create Footnote

1. Place insertion point where footnote reference number will be inserted.

2. Select **L**ayout menu .... **Alt** + **L**

3. Select **F**ootnote .... **F**

4. Select **C**reate .... **C**

5. Type footnote .... **text**

6. Select **C**lose to save footnote and return to document .... **Alt** + **C**

WordPerfect inserts footnote number in document and renumbers existing footnotes automatically.

Edit Footnote

1. Select **L**ayout menu .... **Alt** + **L**

2. Select **F**ootnote .... **F**

3. Select **E**dit .... **E**

4. Type number of footnote to edit .... **number**

5. Select **OK** .... **⏎**

6. Edit footnote.

7. Select desired option(s):

   • Note N**u**mber .... **Alt** + **U** to insert footnote number.

   • **P**revious Number .... **Alt** + **P** to edit previous footnote.

   • **N**ext Number .... **Alt** + **N** to edit next footnote.

8. Select **C**lose to save footnote(s) and return to document .... **Alt** + **C**

FOOTNOTE (continued)

Delete Footnote

- Delete [Footnote:#] code (see DELETE CODES on page 23).

NOTE: *When you delete a footnote, WordPerfect automatically renumbers remaining footnotes.*

Renumber Footnotes

Renumbers footnotes from insertion point forward.

1. Place insertion point where new numbering will begin.
2. Select **L**ayout menu .... **Alt** + **L**
3. Select **F**ootnote .... **F**
4. Select **N**ew Number .... **N**
5. Type new number .... **number**
6. Select **OK** .... **↵**

FOOTNOTE OPTIONS

Changes made affect all footnotes.

Continuous Footnotes

Sets the minimum number of inches a footnote will occupy before WordPerfect will split a footnote across a page.

1. Select **L**ayout menu .... **Alt** + **L**
2. Select **F**ootnote .... **F**
3 Select **O**ptions .... **O**
4. Select Minimum Note **H**eight text box .... **Alt** + **H**
5. Type height (inches) .... **number**
6. If desired, select ☐Print (Continued...) **M**essage . **Alt** + **M**
7. Select **OK** .... **↵**

88

Footnote Number Style and Appearance

Sets the numbering style and appearance of footnotes from insertion point forward.

1. Select <u>L</u>ayout menu .... `Alt`+`L`
2. Select <u>F</u>ootnote .... `F`
3. Select <u>O</u>ptions .... `O`
4. Open N<u>u</u>mbering Method `[    ▼]` ..... `Alt`+`U`, `F4`

   <u>and</u> select desired numbering style:

   - <u>N</u>umbers — marks footnotes with numbers ...... `N`
   - <u>L</u>etters — marks footnotes with letters .... `L`
   - <u>C</u>haracters — marks footnotes with characters .... `C`

     If <u>C</u>haracters was selected,

     a) Select <u>C</u>haracters text box .... `Alt`+`C`
     b) Type desired character(s) to
        use for footnote numbering .... **character**

        NOTE: Character(s) is used once, then doubled, tripled, etc.

   To edit footnote numbering style in <u>document text</u>:

   a) Select Style in <u>T</u>ext text box .... `Alt`+`T`
   b) If necessary, place insertion point and/or delete codes.
   c) Open Style in <u>T</u>ext `◄` .... `F4`

      <u>and</u> select desired text style .... **letter**

      <u>N</u>ote Number, <u>B</u>old, <u>U</u>nderline, <u>D</u>ouble Underline, <u>I</u>talics, <u>O</u>utline, Shado<u>w</u>, S<u>m</u>all Caps, <u>R</u>edline, <u>S</u>trikeout, Su<u>p</u>erscript, Sub<u>s</u>cript, <u>F</u>ine, <u>S</u>mall, <u>L</u>arge, <u>V</u>ery Large, E<u>x</u>tra Large

   d) Repeat steps b and c as needed.

Continued ...

FOOTNOTE OPTIONS (continued)

To edit footnote numbering style in <u>footnote text</u>:

a) Select Style in <u>N</u>ote text box . . . . `Alt`+`N`

b) If necessary, place insertion point and/or delete codes.

c) Open Style in <u>N</u>ote `◄` . . . . `F4`

   <u>and</u> select desired text style . . . . **letter**

   *<u>N</u>ote Number, <u>B</u>old, <u>U</u>nderline, <u>D</u>ouble Underline,
   <u>I</u>talics, <u>O</u>utline, Shado<u>w</u>, S<u>m</u>all Caps, <u>R</u>edline,
   <u>S</u>trikeout, Sup<u>e</u>rscript, Subs<u>c</u>ript, <u>F</u>ine, <u>S</u>mall,
   <u>L</u>arge, <u>V</u>ery Large, E<u>x</u>tra Large*

d) Repeat steps b and c as needed.

To restart footnote number on each page:

• Select ☐<u>R</u>estart Numbering
  on Each Page . . . . `Alt`+`R`

5. Select OK . . . . `↵`

Other Footnote Options

*Sets footnote spacing, position, and separators from insertion
point forward.*

1. Select <u>L</u>ayout menu . . . . `Alt`+`L`

2. Select <u>F</u>ootnote . . . . `F`

3. Select <u>O</u>ptions . . . . `O`

To set line spacing in footnote:

a) Select <u>L</u>ine Spacing in Notes text box . . . . . . `Alt`+`L`

b) Type number (inches) . . . . **number**

To set spacing between footnotes:

a) Select Spacing <u>B</u>etween Notes text box . . . . `Alt`+`B`

b) Type number (inches) . . . . **number**

To position footnote on page:

• Open <u>P</u>osition ☐   ♦ . . . . `Alt`+`P`, `F4`

   <u>and</u> select desired position . . . . **letter**

   <u>A</u>fter text, <u>B</u>ottom of Page

Continued ...

FOOTNOTE OPTIONS (continued)

To change footnote separator:

- Open **S**eparator [⬚ ⬍] . . . . **Alt** + **S** , **F4**

  <u>and</u> select desired separator . . . . **letter**

  <u>N</u>o line, 2-<u>i</u>nch line, <u>M</u>argin to Margin

4. Select **OK** . . . . **↵**

GENERATE

Generates tables of contents, tables of authorities, lists, cross-references,
indexes, and endnote placement codes.

NOTE: *Before using Generate, you must first mark text and insert*
define codes. If generating endnotes, insert Endnote
Placement code. See specific topics for additional
information. If you edit your document, you may need to
generate the data again.

1. Select **T**ools menu . . . . **Alt** + **T**

2. Select Ge**n**erate (*WP5.2*) . . . . **N**

   OR   **OR**

   Select **G**enerate (*WP5.1*) . . . . **G**

   NOTE: *The message "Generate updates all Lists, Indexes,*
   ToCs, ToAs, Cross-References, and Endnote
   Placement codes. Continue" appears.

3. Select **Y**es . . . . **↵**

GO TO

Moves the insertion point to a specific page, top or bottom of a page, a specific column within a set of columns, or to a specific cell or column within a table.

Go to Specific Page

1. Select Edit menu . . . . `Alt`+`E`

2. Select Go To . . . . `G`

3. Type page number in Go To Page Number
   text box . . . . **number**

4. Select OK . . . . `↵`

Go to Top or Bottom of Current Page

1. Select Edit menu . . . . `Alt`+`E`

2. Select Go To . . . . `G`

3. Open Position [____ ‡] . . . . `Alt`+`P`, `F4`

   and select desired position . . . . **letter**
   Top of Current Page, Bottom of Current Page

4. Select OK . . . . `↵`

Go to Previous Insertion Point Position

1. Select Edit menu . . . . `Alt`+`E`

2. Select Go To . . . . `G`

3. Select Last Position . . . . `Alt`+`L`

GO TO (continued)

Go to Column or Position in Column

1. Place insertion point in any column.

2. Select Edit menu . . . . `Alt`+`E`

3. Select Go To . . . . `G`

4. Open Position [____ ⬧] . . . . `Alt`+`P`, `F4`

   and select desired position . . . . **letter**

   Top of Column, Bottom of Column, Previous Column,
   Next Column, First Column, Last Column

5. Select **OK** . . . . `⏎`

Go to Position in Table

1. Place insertion point in table.

2. Select Edit menu . . . . `Alt`+`E`

3. Select Go To . . . . `G`

4. Open Position [____ ⬧] . . . . `Alt`+`P`, `F4`

   and select desired position . . . . **letter**

   Go to Cell, Top of Cell, Bottom of Cell, First Cell,
   Last Cell, Top of Column, Bottom of Column, Previous Column,
   Next Column, First Column, Last Column

5. Select **OK** to move to specified location . . . . `⏎`

Go to Beginning of Selection or Restore Previous Text Selection

1. Select Edit menu . . . . `Alt`+`E`

2. Select Go To . . . . `G`

3. Open Position [____ ⬧] . . . . `Alt`+`P`, `F4`

   and select desired position . . . . **letter**

   Beginning of Selection, Reselect Text

4. Select **OK** to move to specified location . . . . `⏎`

GRAMMATIK — CHECK DOCUMENT *WP5.2*

1. If checking part of a document, select text (page 218) to check.

2. Select **T**ools menu . . . . `Alt`+`T`

3. Select **G**rammatik . . . . `G`

4. When Grammatik finds a problem, select desired option:

   - **C**lose   ends proofreading session.
   - **I**gnore Class   turns off rule class for current item.
   - Ignore **P**hrase   ignores all instances of phrase for this session.
   - **L**earn Word   adds highlighted word to Grammatik's dictionary.
   - **M**ark Problem   inserts suggestion in document and encloses it with square brackets.
   - **R**eplace   replaces highlighted item with suggested item.
   - Replace/Ne**x**t   replaces highlighted item and continues proofreading.
   - **W**riting Guide   provides general writing help.
   - **N**ext Problem   ignores current item only and continues proofreading.

   NOTE: When Grammatik completes proofreading, it displays the message: "Checking complete. Save changes to this document?"

5. Select one option:

   - **S**ave . . . . `S`
     to save edited file with same name as original file.
     Original file is renamed with a .GBK file extension.

   - Save **A**s . . . . `A`
     to save edited file with filename you specify.

     a) Type filename . . . . **filename**

     b) Select **OK** . . . . `↵`

   - **D**iscard . . . . `D`, `Y`
     to discard changes to document and confirm.

6. Select **N**o when prompted to paste text . . . . `N`
   NOTE: This prompt applies only to text checked in the Clipboard.

GRAPHICS BOX

There are five types of graphics boxes: Figure, Text, Equation, Table and User. Although you can put any kind of data in any type of graphics box, by default, WordPerfect opens specific editors for <u>*some*</u> *box types when your create them:*

- *Figure graphics box — opens Figure Editor;*
- *Equation graphics box — opens Equation Editor;*
- *Text graphics box — opens Text Box Editor.*

For Table or User graphics boxes, you must select an editor.

WordPerfect automatically numbers each graphics box type separately. Each box type has its own default borders style, border spacing, and grey shading. All graphics box types are initially anchored to a page position.

Create Graphics Box

Also see Retrieve a Graphic File Directly into a Document on next page.

1. Place insertion point where graphics box will be inserted.

2. Select **G**raphics menu .... **Alt** + **G**

3. Select one box type:

   - **F**igure .... **F**
   - Text **B**ox .... **B**
   - **E**quation .... **E**
   - **T**able Box .... **T**
   - **U**ser Box .... **U**

4. Select **C**reate .... **C**

   If Table Box or User Box was selected,
   a) Select one editor type:

   O **F**igure Editor .... **F**

   O **T**ext Editor .... **T**

   O **E**quation Editor .... **E**

   b) Select **OK** .... **↵**

5. Refer to the section for the editor you are using:
   - *GRAPHICS BOX — FIGURE EDITOR on pages 107-113.*
   - *GRAPHICS BOX — TEXT BOX EDITOR on page 114.*
   - *GRAPHICS BOX — EQUATION EDITOR on pages 115-117.*

GRAPHICS BOX (continued)

Retrieve a Graphic File Directly into a Document

Retrieves a graphic file stored on disk into a <u>figure box</u> and inserts it directly into your document. Also see Create Graphics Box on previous page.

1. Place insertion point where graphics box will be inserted.

2. Select Graphics menu . . . . **Alt** + **G**

3. Select Figure . . . . **F**

4. Select Retrieve . . . . **R**

5. Select desired file in Files list box . . . . . **Alt** + **I**, **↹**
   See DIRECTORIES — LOCATING FILES, page 25.

6. Select Retrieve . . . . **↵**

Select a Graphics Box

• Click on graphic box.

   OR

   If Wrap Text Around Box is off (page 106),

   a) Point to graphics box and click right mouse button.

   b) Click on . . . . **Select Box**

Edit Graphics Box with Mouse

Also see Edit Graphics Box using Menu on next page.

1. Double-click on graphics box to edit.

   OR

   Point to graphics box to edit.

   a) Click right mouse button.

   b) Click on . . . . **Edit *box type***
      *Where **box type** is the name of the graphics box type you are editing.*

2. Edit contents of graphics box.

   Refer to the section for the editor you are using:
   • *GRAPHICS BOX — FIGURE EDITOR on pages 107-113.*
   • *GRAPHICS BOX — TEXT BOX EDITOR on page 114.*
   • *GRAPHICS BOX — EQUATION EDITOR on pages 115-117.*

96

GRAPHICS BOX (continued)

Edit Graphics Box using Menu

Also see Edit Graphics Box with Mouse on previous page.

1. If necessary, turn Reveal Codes on . . . . **Alt** + **F3**

2. Highlight code of graphics box to edit.

3. Select **G**raphics menu . . . . **Alt** + **G**

4. Select the graphics box type:

   - **F**igure . . . . **F**
   - Text **B**ox . . . . **B**
   - **E**quation . . . . **E**
   - **T**able Box . . . . **T**
   - **U**ser Box . . . . **U**

5. Select **E**dit . . . . **E**

6. If necessary, type box number to edit . . . . **number**

7. Select **OK** . . . . ↵

8. Edit contents of graphics box.

   Refer to the section for the editor you are using:
   - *GRAPHICS BOX — FIGURE EDITOR on pages 107-113.*
   - *GRAPHICS BOX — TEXT BOX EDITOR on page 114.*
   - *GRAPHICS BOX — EQUATION EDITOR on pages 115-117.*

GRAPHICS BOX (continued)

Delete Graphics Box

- Delete graphics box code (see DELETE CODES on page 23).

OR

1. Click on graphic box to delete.

    OR

    If Wrap Text Around Box is off (page 106),

    a) Point to graphics box and click right mouse button.

    b) Click on . . . . **S̲elect Box**

2. Press **Delete** . . . . `Del`

*NOTE: When you delete a graphics box, WordPerfect renumbers
remaining graphics boxes of the same type, automatically.*

Renumber Graphics Box Type

*All graphics boxes of specified type will be renumbered from
insertion point forward.*

1. If necessary, turn Reveal Codes on . . . . `Alt`+`F3`

2. Highlight code of graphics box to renumber.

3. Select G̲raphics menu . . . . `Alt`+`G`

4. Select the graphics box type . . . . **letter**
    F̲igure, Text B̲ox, E̲quation, T̲able Box, U̲ser Box

5. Select N̲ew Number . . . . `N`

6. Type new number . . . . **number**

7. Select OK . . . . `⏎`

GRAPHICS BOX (continued)

Move and Size a Graphics Box with Mouse

NOTE: *You cannot move a graphics box if it is anchored to a character*
(page 104). Moving a graphics box will not change the position
of the graphics box code.

- Click on graphic box to move or size.
  A dashed border with sizing handles appears around graphics box.
  OR

  If Wrap Text Around Box is off (page 106),

  a) Point to graphics box and click right mouse button.

  b) Click on . . . . **S̲elect Box**
  A dashed border with sizing handles appears around graphics box.

To move graphics box:

  a) Place mouse pointer in graphics box.
  Pointer becomes a ⊕.

  b) Drag box outline to desired position.

To size graphics box:

  a) Place mouse pointer on any sizing handle.
  Pointer becomes a ⬉ ⬍ ⬌.

  b) Drag box outline until desired size is obtained.

GRAPHICS BOX (continued)

Add or Edit Caption for a Graphics Box Type

1. • Place mouse pointer on graphics box
     <u>and</u> click the right mouse button.

   • Click on .... **Edit Ca̲ption...**

   • Go to step 2.

OR

1. • If necessary, turn Reveal Codes on ...... `Alt`+`F3`

   • Highlight desired graphics box code.

   • Select G̲raphics menu .... `Alt`+`G`

   • Select the graphics box type .... **letter**
     F̲igure, Text B̲ox, E̲quation, T̲able Box, U̲ser Box

   • Select Ca̲ption .... `A`

   • If necessary, type number of graphics box ... **number**

   • Select **OK** .... `⏎`

   *By default, WordPerfect includes the box type and number code
   (i.e., Figure 1) in caption.*

2. Add or edit caption text or codes.

   To insert the graphics box number code:

   a) Place insertion point where graphics box number
      code will be inserted.

   b) Select Box N̲umber .... `Alt`+`N`

3. Select C̲lose .... `Alt`+`C`

GRAPHICS BOX (continued)

Caption Options for a Graphics Box Type

Changes caption position, numbering style, format style, and provides for second-level numbering. Changes will affect all graphics boxes of the same type from the insertion point forward.

1. If necessary, turn Reveal Codes on .... `Alt`+`F3`

2. Highlight code of first graphics box to change.

3. Select **G**raphics menu .... `Alt`+`G`

4. Select the graphics box type .... **letter**
   Figure, Text Box, Equation, Table Box, User Box

5. Select **O**ptions .... `O`

   To change caption position:

   • Open Caption **P**osition [　　♦] .... `Alt`+`P`, `F4`
     and select desired position .... **letter**
     *Below-Outside, Above-Outside, Below-Inside, Above-Inside
     for Equation graphics boxes:
     Below, Above, Left, Right*

   To change first-level caption numbering:

   • Open **F**irst Level [　　♦] .... `Alt`+`F`, `F4`
     and select desired numbering method .... **letter**
     Off, Numbers, Letters, Roman Numerals

   To create second-level caption numbering:

   a) Open Se**c**ond Level [　　♦] ...... `Alt`+`C`, `F4`
      and select desired numbering method .... **letter**
      Off, Numbers, Letters, Roman Numerals

   b) Place insertion point after "1"
      in **S**tyle text box .... `Alt`+`S`, `↴`
      NOTE: *Number one represents first-level numbering.*

   c) Type a character (such as a dash (-),
      a decimal point (.), etc.)
      to separate the two numbering levels ..... **character**

   d) Type **2** (second-level numbering) .... `2`

Continued ...

GRAPHICS BOX — Caption Options for a Graphics Box (continued)

To change caption number text and appearance:

a) Select **S**tyle text box . . . .   **Alt** + **S**

b) If desired, delete existing codes . . . .   **⇄** , **Del**

c) If desired, type new text for caption number . . . .   **text**

> **NOTE:** *Use numbers 1 and 2 to specify placement of numbering levels (i.e., ART 1-2).*

d) If desired, place insertion point where format code will be placed . . . .   **⇄**

   • Open **S**tyle **◁** **F4**

     and select desired text style . . . . **letter**

     *B*old, *I*talics, *U*nderline, Small *C*aps

e) Repeat steps b-d as needed.

> **Example:** *[Italic On][Bold On]ART 1-2[Bold Off][Italic Off]*

6. Select **OK** . . . .   **⏎**

102

Appearance Options for a Graphics Box Type

Changes border style and spacing, background shading, and controls how graphics boxes are paged. Changes will affect all graphics boxes of the same type from the insertion point forward.

1. If necessary, turn Reveal Codes on . . . . `Alt`+`F3`
2. Highlight code of first graphics box to change.
3. Select **G**raphics menu . . . . `Alt`+`G`
4. Select the graphics box type . . . . **letter**
   *F*igure, Text *B*ox, *E*quation, *T*able Box, *U*ser Box
5. Select **O**ptions . . . . `O`

   To change border style:
   a) Open a **B**order Styles [____ ♦] . . . . `Alt`+letter, `F4`
      *L*eft, *R*ight, *T*op, *B*ottom
      and select desired style . . . . **letter**
      *N*one, *S*ingle, *D*ouble, *D*ashed, *D*otted, *T*hick, *E*xtra Thick

   b) Repeat step a for each border to change.

   To change border spacing:
   a) Select desired border's text box . . . `Alt`+letter, `Tab`
      *L*eft, *R*ight, *T*op, *B*ottom
      Press Tab until desired text box is selected.

   b) Type distance (inches) from border . . . . **number**
   c) Repeat steps a and b for each border to change.

   To set background shading:
   a) Select **G**ray Shading increment box . . . . . . `Alt`+`G`
   b) Type percentage of black (0-100) . . . . **number**

   To set minimum offset from paragraph:
   a) Select Mi**n**imum Offset
      from Paragraph text box . . . . `Alt`+`N`
   b) Type offset distance (inches) . . . . **number**

6. Select **OK** . . . . `↵`

GRAPHICS BOX — BOX POSITION AND SIZE

Open Box Position and Size Dialog Box

Opens the Box Position and Size dialog box from which you can:

- *Anchor and Position a Graphics Box;*
- *Change Graphics Box Type;*
- *Size a Graphics Box;*
- *Set How Text Wraps Around a Graphics Box.*

Also see Move and Size a Graphics Box with Mouse on page 98.

1. Place mouse pointer on graphics box <u>and</u> click the right mouse button.

2. Click on .... **Box Position...**

   FROM BOX POSITION AND SIZE DIALOG BOX

   See the following topics:

   - *Anchor and Position a Graphics Box on page 104.*
   - *Change Graphics Box Type on page 105.*
   - *Size a Graphics Box on page 106.*
   - *Set How Text Wraps Around a Graphics Box on page 106.*

OR

1. If necessary, turn Reveal Codes on .... `Alt`+`F3`

2. Highlight desired graphics box code.

3. Select <u>G</u>raphics menu .... `Alt`+`G`

4. Select the graphics box type .... **letter**
   <u>F</u>igure, Text <u>B</u>ox, <u>E</u>quation, <u>T</u>able Box, <u>U</u>ser Box

5. Select <u>P</u>osition .... `P`

6. If necessary, type number of graphics box ..... **number**

7. Select OK .... `⏎`

   FROM BOX POSITION AND SIZE DIALOG BOX

   See the following topics:

   - *Anchor and Position a Graphics Box on page 104.*
   - *Change Graphics Box Type on page 105.*
   - *Size a Graphics Box on page 106.*
   - *Set How Text Wraps Around a Graphics Box on page 106.*

104

Anchor and Position a Graphics Box

Also see Move and Size a Graphics Box with Mouse on page 98.

1. Open "Box Position and Size" dialog box for graphics box to change (page 103).

FROM BOX POSITION AND SIZE DIALOG BOX

To change <u>anchor type</u>:

- Open <u>A</u>nchor To [⬦] . . . . `Alt`+`A`, `F4`
  <u>and</u> select desired anchor type . . . . **letter**
  <u>P</u>aragraph, Pa<u>g</u>e, <u>C</u>haracter

To set <u>vertical position</u> when anchored to <u>character</u>:

- Open <u>V</u>ertical Position [⬦] . . . . `Alt`+`V`, `F4`
  <u>and</u> select desired position . . . . **letter**
  <u>T</u>op, <u>C</u>enter, <u>B</u>ottom, B<u>a</u>seline

To set <u>vertical position</u> when anchored to a <u>paragraph</u>:

a) Select Vertical <u>P</u>osition text box . . . . `Alt`+`P`

b) Type offset from top of paragraph . . . . **number**

To set <u>horizontal position</u> when anchored to <u>paragraph</u>:

- Open <u>H</u>orizontal Position [⬦] . . . `Alt`+`H`, `F4`
  <u>and</u> select desired position . . . . **letter**
  *Margin-<u>L</u>eft, Margin-<u>R</u>ight, Margin-<u>C</u>enter, Margin-<u>F</u>ull,
  <u>S</u>et Position*

  If <u>S</u>et Position was selected,

  1) Select P<u>o</u>sition text box . . . . `Alt`+`O`

  2) Type distance from left edge of page . . . . **number**

To set <u>vertical position</u> when anchored to <u>page</u>:

- Open <u>V</u>ertical Position [⬦] . . . . `Alt`+`V`, `F4`
  <u>and</u> select desired position . . . . **letter**
  <u>F</u>ull Page, <u>T</u>op, <u>C</u>enter, <u>B</u>ottom, <u>S</u>et Position

  If <u>S</u>et Position was selected,

  1) Select <u>P</u>osition text box . . . . `Alt`+`P`

  2) Type distance from top of page . . . . **number**

Continued ...

GRAPHICS BOX — BOX POSITION AND SIZE
— Anchor and Position a Graphics Box (continued)

To set <u>horizontal position</u> when anchored to <u>page</u>:

- Open **H**orizontal Position [⬍] . . . **Alt** + **H** , **F4**
  <u>and</u> select desired position . . . . **letter**
  Margin-<u>L</u>eft, Margin-<u>R</u>ight, Margin-<u>C</u>enter, Margin-<u>F</u>ull,
  Column-<u>L</u>eft, Column-<u>R</u>ight, Column-Ce<u>n</u>ter, Column-F<u>u</u>ll,
  <u>S</u>et Position

If <u>S</u>et Position was selected,

1) Select P<u>o</u>sition text box . . . . **Alt** + **O**

2) Type offset from top of page . . . . **number**

**To set number of <u>pages to skip</u> when anchored
to <u>page</u>:**

a) Select Number of Pages <u>t</u>o Skip text box . . **Alt** + **T**

b) Type number of pages . . . . **number**

2. Select **OK** . . . . ⏎

Change Graphics Box Type

Changes graphics box type without changing its contents.

1. Open "Box Position and Size" dialog box for graphics box
   to change (page 103).

FROM BOX POSITION AND SIZE DIALOG BOX

2. Open **B**ox Type [⬍] . . . . **Alt** + **B** , **F4**
   <u>and</u> select desired graphics box type . . . . **letter**
   <u>F</u>igure, <u>T</u>able Box, Text <u>B</u>ox, <u>U</u>ser Box, <u>E</u>quation

3. Select **OK** . . . . ⏎

106

Size a Graphics Box

Also see Move and Size a Graphics Box with Mouse on page 98.

1. Open "Box Position and Size" dialog box for graphics box to change (page 103).

FROM BOX POSITION AND SIZE DIALOG BOX

2. Open Size [⬚ ⬩] . . . . `Alt`+`S`, `F4`
   <u>and</u> select desired option:

   - Auto Both . . . . `A`
   - Auto Width . . . . `W`
     a) Select Height text box . . . . `Alt`+`E`
     b) Type height (inches) . . . . **number**
   - Auto Height . . . . `H`
     a) Select Width text box . . . . `Alt`+`W`
     b) Type width (inches) . . . . **number**
   - Set Both . . . . `S`
     a) Select Width text box . . . . `Alt`+`W`
     b) Type width (inches) . . . . **number**
     c) Select Height text box . . . . `Alt`+`E`
     d) Type height (inches) . . . . **number**

3. Select **OK** . . . . `⏎`

Set How Text Wraps Around a Graphics Box

1. Open "Box Position and Size" dialog box for graphics box to change (page 103).

FROM BOX POSITION AND SIZE DIALOG BOX

2. Select or clear ☐Wrap Text Around Box . . . . `Alt`+`R`
3. Select **OK** . . . . `⏎`

GRAPHICS BOX — FIGURE EDITOR

When you create (page 94) or edit (pages 95 and 96) a graphics box that contains a graphic file, WordPerfect opens the Figure Editor.

Retrieve Graphic File into Figure Editor

NOTE: Replaces existing graphic in graphics box if one exists.
FROM FIGURE EDITOR

1. Click on .... [Retrieve]

   OR

   Select File menu .... **Alt**+**F**

   • Select Retrieve .... **R**

2. Select desired file in Files list box ...... **Alt**+**I**, **↕**

   See DIRECTORIES — LOCATING FILES, page 25.

3. Select Retrieve .... **↵**

4. Select another option or select **Close** .... **Alt**+**F**, **C**

Save Contents of Figure Editor to a File

Saves graphic, in WordPerfect graphics format, to a file on disk.
FROM FIGURE EDITOR

1. Select File menu .... **Alt**+**F**

2. Select Save As .... **A**

3. Type a filename in Save As text box .... **filename**

4. Select Save .... **↵**

   If replace warning box appears,

   • Select Yes .... **Y**
     to overwrite existing file with current figure.

   OR   **OR**

   Select No .... **N**
     to return to Save As dialog box

5. Select another option or select **Close** .... **Alt**+**F**, **C**

108

Store Graphic Apart from Document

Stores the graphic in the graphics box apart from the document. This reduces the size of your document but can increase the time it takes to print and preview the document.

FROM FIGURE EDITOR

1. Select File menu .... **Alt** + **F**
2. Select Graphic On Disk .... **G**
3. Type a filename in Save As text box .... **filename**

   NOTE: If necessary, type path to desired directory.
4. Select Save .... **↵**
5. Select another option or select Close .... **Alt** + **F**, **C**

Box Position and Size Options from Figure Editor

FROM FIGURE EDITOR

1. Click on .... **Fig Pos**

   OR

   Select File menu .... **Alt** + **F**
   - Select Box Position .... **P**
2. Change settings as desired.

   See GRAPHICS BOX — BOX POSITION AND SIZE on pages 104-106.
3. Select OK .... **↵**
4. Select another option or select Close .... **Alt** + **F**, **C**

Change Colors of Figure to Black and White

FROM FIGURE EDITOR

1. Select Edit menu .... **Alt** + **E**
2. Select Black and White .... **B**

NOTE: Repeat steps to return figure to color.

GRAPHICS BOX — FIGURE EDITOR (continued)

Edit All Figure Options

Moves, scales, and rotates figure a specific amount. Changes appearance of figure and allows you to see effects of changes.

FROM FIGURE EDITOR

1. Click on .... 🔲 Edit All

   OR

   Select <u>E</u>dit menu .... `Alt`+`E`

   • Select <u>E</u>dit All .... `E`

   To move figure a specified amount:

   a) Select <u>H</u>orizontal increment box .... `Alt`+`H`

   b) Type distance (inches) .... **number**

   c) Select <u>V</u>ertical increment box .... `Alt`+`V`

   d) Type distance (inches) .... **number**

   NOTE: Positive numbers move figure up and to the right. Negative numbers move figure down and to the left. The specified measurements move figure from its original position.

   To scale figure a specified amount:

   a) Select Scale <u>X</u> increment box .... `Alt`+`X`
   to scale figure horizontally.

   b) Type percentage (0-999%) .... **number**

   c) Select Scale <u>Y</u> increment box .... `Alt`+`Y`
   to scale figure vertically.

   d) Type percentage (0-999%) .... **number**

   To rotate figure a specified amount:

   a) Select <u>R</u>otate increment box .... `Alt`+`R`

   b) Type degrees (0-360) .... **number**

   NOTE: Number represents degrees in counter-clockwise direction.

Continued ...

110

To flip figure on its vertical axis:

- Select ☐Mirror Image . . . . `Alt`+`M`

To display figure as line drawing:

- Select ☐Outline . . . . `Alt`+`O`

To display complementary color of each pixel:

- Select ☐Invert . . . . `Alt`+`I`

   NOTE: *Invert does not affect figures that are black and white.*

To display figure in black and white:

- Select ☐Black and White . . . . `Alt`+`B`

To preview changes:

- Select Apply . . . . `Alt`+`A`

2. Select OK . . . . `↵`

Invert Figure

Displays the complementary color of each pixel in figure.
FROM FIGURE EDITOR

1. Select Edit menu . . . . `Alt`+`E`
2. Select Invert . . . . `I`

NOTE: *Repeat steps to return figure to original color.*

Mirror a Figure

Flips figure on its vertical axis.
FROM FIGURE EDITOR

- Click on . . . . `▶◀ Mirror`

OR

1. Select Edit menu . . . . `Alt`+`E`
2. Select Mirror . . . . `M`

GRAPHICS BOX — FIGURE EDITOR (continued)

Move Figure

FROM FIGURE EDITOR

1. Click on .... | ⌨ Move |

2. Point to any part of figure.
   Point to a part of figure that will act as a reference point for move.

3. Drag ✛ to new position.
   "Pos X" and "Y" numbers on status bar indicate change of position.

OR

1. Select **E**dit menu .... **Alt** + **E**

2. Select Mo**v**e .... **V**

3. Press **Ins** until desired percentage to
   move figure appears on status bar .... **Ins**

4. Press arrow keys until desired location is obtained ... **↕**

Outline a Figure

Displays the figure as a line drawing.
FROM FIGURE EDITOR

• Click on .... | ☑ Outline |

OR

1. Select **E**dit menu .... **Alt** + **E**

2. Select **O**utline .... **O**

NOTE: *Repeat step(s) to reset figure to color.*

Reset All Changes to a Figure

FROM FIGURE EDITOR

• Click on .... | ⟳ Reset All |

OR

1. Select **E**dit menu .... **Alt** + **E**

2. Select Reset **A**ll .... **A**

GRAPHICS BOX — FIGURE EDITOR (continued)

Rotate Figure

FROM FIGURE EDITOR

1. Click on .... `⟳ Rotate`
   A rotation angle appears.

2. Drag the right end of any axis the desired number of degrees.

OR

1. Select **E**dit menu .... `Alt`+`E`

2. Select **R**otate .... `R`
   A rotation angle appears.

3. Press **Ins** until desired rotate
   percentage appears on status bar .... `Ins`

4. Press **Ctrl + Right Arrow** to rotate
   figure clockwise .... `Ctrl`+`→`

   OR   **OR**

   Press **Ctrl + Left Arrow** to rotate
   figure counter-clockwise .... `Ctrl`+`←`

Scale Figure

FROM FIGURE EDITOR

1. Press **Ins** until desired percentage to scale
   figure appears on status bar .... `Ins`

2. Select **E**dit menu .... `Alt`+`E`

3. Select **S**cale .... `S`

4. Select Enlar**g**e % .... `G`

   OR   **OR**

   Select Re**d**uce % .... `D`

GRAPHICS BOX — FIGURE EDITOR (continued)

Reset Size of Figure

FROM FIGURE EDITOR

- Click on .... $\boxed{\begin{array}{c} ⇧\ ◢\ ⬇ \\ \text{ResetSize} \end{array}}$

OR

1. Select <u>E</u>dit menu .... $\boxed{\text{Alt}}$ + $\boxed{\text{E}}$
2. Select <u>S</u>cale .... $\boxed{\text{S}}$
3. Select <u>R</u>eset Size .... $\boxed{\text{R}}$

Enlarge Figure (Crop)

FROM FIGURE EDITOR

1. Click on .... $\boxed{\begin{array}{c} ⬀ \\ \text{Enlarge} \end{array}}$

    OR

    Select <u>E</u>dit menu .... $\boxed{\text{Alt}}$ + $\boxed{\text{E}}$

    a) Select <u>S</u>cale .... $\boxed{\text{S}}$

    b) Select <u>E</u>nlarge Area .... $\boxed{\text{E}}$

    A ▷ and cross lines appear.

2. Place pointer on upper-left portion of figure to enlarge.

3. Drag selection rectangle over area to enlarge.

GRAPHICS BOX — TEXT BOX EDITOR

When you create (page 94) or edit (pages 95 and 96) a graphics box that contains text, WordPerfect opens the Text Box Editor. From this editor you have most of the features that WordPerfect normally provides. In this section we will show you the features that are unique to the Text Box Editor.

Box Position and Size Options from Text Box Editor

FROM TEXT BOX EDITOR

1. Select Box Position . . . . **Alt** + **P**

2. Change settings as desired.
   See GRAPHICS BOX — BOX POSITION AND SIZE on pages 104-106.

3. Select OK . . . . **↵**

4. Select another option or select Close . . . . **Alt** + **C**

Rotate Text in Text Box

NOTE: Your printer must support rotated fonts. Rotated text will not appear rotated in document window.

FROM TEXT BOX EDITOR

1. Select Rotate . . . . **Alt** + **R**

2. Select desired rotation . . . . **character**
   Rotate None, Rotate 90%, Rotate 180%, Rotate 270%

3. Select OK . . . . **↵**

4. Select another option or select Close . . . . **Alt** + **C**

GRAPHICS BOX — EQUATION EDITOR

When you create (page 94) or edit (pages 95 and 96) a graphics box that contains an equation, WordPerfect opens the Equation Editor. With the Equation Editor, you can create and edit mathematical or scientific equations. The Equation Editor displays three main areas:

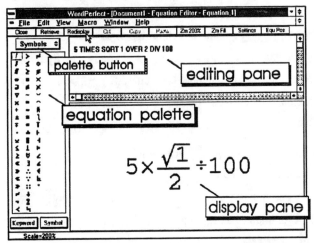

- *In the **editing pane** you type or paste numbers and other expressions.*
- *In the **equation palette** you select items to paste into the editing pane.*
- *You can open the **palette button** and select one the following sets of symbols and commands:*
  Commands, Large, Symbols, Greek, Arrows, Sets, Other, Function
- *You can select the **Redisplay** button and WordPerfect will draw the formula in the **display pane**.*

Create a Sample Equation with Mouse

FROM EQUATION EDITOR

1. In editing pane, type 5 .... **5**
2. Open [⬍] (palette button) at top of palette
   and select .... **Symbols**
3. In equation palette, double-click on .... **X**
4. Open [⬍] (palette button) at top of palette
   and select .... **Commands**

Continued ...

116

5. In equation palette, double-click on .... **SQRT**

6. In editing pane, type 1 .... **1**

7. In equation palette, double-click on .... **OVER**

8. In editing pane, type 2 .... **2**

9. Open `[    ▼ ]` (palette button) at top of palette

    <u>and</u> select .... **Symbols**

10. In equation palette, double-click on .... **÷**

11. In editing pane, type 100 .... **100**

12. Click on .... `Redisplay`

Equation Font Size and Alignment

FROM EQUATION EDITOR

1. Select <u>F</u>ile menu .... `Alt` + `F`

2. Select <u>S</u>ettings .... `S`

    To set font size:

    a) Select ○ <u>P</u>oint Size .... `Alt` + `P`

    b) Select increment box .... `Tab`

    c) Type font size .... **number**

    To change alignment:

    • Open <u>H</u>orizontal `[    ▼ ]` .... `Alt` + `H`, `F4`

    and select desired position in box .... **letter**
    <u>L</u>eft, <u>C</u>enter, <u>R</u>ight

    AND/OR   **AND/OR**

    Open <u>V</u>ertical `[    ▼ ]` .... `Alt` + `V`, `F4`

    and select desired position in box .... **letter**
    <u>T</u>op, <u>C</u>enter, <u>B</u>ottom

3. Select **OK** .... `↵`

4. Select another option or select **Close** .... `Alt` + `F`, `C`

GRAPHICS BOX — EQUATION EDITOR (continued)

Enlarge or Reduce Equation View in Display Pane

Changes the size of equation in display pane, but not in your document.
FROM EQUATION EDITOR

1. Select View menu .... Alt + V
2. Select desired percentage or zoom command ... character
   100%, 200%, Zoom In, Zoom Out,
   Zoom Area, Zoom Fill
3. Select another option or select **Close** .... Alt + F , C

Box Position and Size Options from Equation Editor

FROM EQUATION EDITOR

1. Select File menu .... Alt + F
2. Select Box Position .... P
3. Change settings as desired.
   See GRAPHICS BOX — BOX POSITION AND SIZE on pages 104-106.
4. Select **OK** .... ↵
5. Select another option or select **Close** .... Alt + F , C

GRAPHICS LINE

Create Horizontal Line

1. Place insertion point where line will be placed.
2. Select **G**raphics menu . . . . **Alt**+**G**
3. Select **L**ine . . . . **L**
4. Select **H**orizontal . . . . **H**

   To set horizontal position of line:

   • Open **H**orizontal Position [⬚ ⬍] . . . **Alt**+**H**, **F4**
   and select desired position . . . . **letter**
   Left, Right, Center, Full, Specify

   If Specify was selected,

   1) Select P**o**sition text box . . . . **Alt**+**O**
   2) Type distance (inches) from
      left edge of page . . . . **number**

   To set vertical position of line:

   • Open **V**ertical Position [⬚ ⬍] . . . . . **Alt**+**V**, **F4**
   and select desired option . . . . **letter**
   Baseline, Specify

   If Specify was selected,

   1) Select **P**osition text box . . . . **Alt**+**P**
   2) Type distance (inches) from
      top edge of page . . . . **number**

   To change line length:

   a) Select **L**ength text box . . . . **Alt**+**L**
   b) Type length (inches) . . . . **number**
      NOTE: *If the horizontal position is set to Full,*
      the length of the line is determined by the
      distance between margins.

GRAPHICS LINE — Create Horizontal Line (continued)

To change <u>line thickness</u>:

a) Select <u>T</u>hickness text box .... **Alt** + **T**

b) Type thickness (inches) .... **number**

> **NOTE:** If the vertical position is set to <u>S</u>pecify,
> the bottom of the line expands downward.
> If it is set to <u>B</u>aseline, the top edge of
> line expands upward.

To change <u>line shading</u>:

a) Select <u>G</u>rey Shading increment box .... **Alt** + **G**

b) Type percent of black (0-100) .... **number**

5. Select **OK** .... **↵**

Create Vertical Line

1. Place insertion point where line will be placed.

2. Select <u>G</u>raphics menu .... **Alt** + **G**

3. Select <u>L</u>ine .... **L**

4. Select <u>V</u>ertical .... **V**

To set <u>horizontal position</u> of line:

• Open <u>H</u>orizontal Position [⬍] ... **Alt** + **H**, **F4**

  <u>and</u> select desired position .... **letter**

  <u>L</u>eft Margin, <u>R</u>ight Margin, <u>B</u>etween Columns, <u>S</u>pecify

  If <u>B</u>etween Columns was selected,

  1) Select <u>R</u>ight of Column
     text box .... **Alt** + **R**

  2) Type column number .... **number**

  If <u>S</u>pecify was selected,

  1) Select P<u>o</u>sition text box. .... **Alt** + **O**

  2) Type distance (inches) from
     left edge of page .... **number**

Continued ...

120

To set <u>vertical position</u> of line:

- Open **V**ertical Position `[____ ⬍]` ..... `Alt`+`V`, `F4`
  and select desired position .... **letter**
  Full Page, Top, Center, Bottom, Specify

  If <u>S</u>pecify was selected,

  1) Select **P**osition text box .... `Alt`+`P`

  2) Type distance (inches) from
     top edge of page .... **number**

To change <u>line length</u>:

a) Select **L**ength text box .... `Alt`+`L`

b) Type length (inches) .... **number**

  > *NOTE: If the horizontal position is set to Full, the length
  > of the line is determined by the distance between
  > margins.*

To change <u>line thickness</u>:

a) Select **T**hickness text box .... `Alt`+`T`

b) Type thickness (inches) .... **number**

  > *NOTE: Vertical lines always expand to the right.*

To change <u>line shading</u>:

a) Select **G**rey Shading increment box ...... `Alt`+`G`

b) Type percent of black (0-100) .... **number**

5. Select **OK** .... `↵`

Move Line with Mouse

1. Click on line to move.
   A dashed border with handles (small squares) appears around line.

2. Point anywhere on line away from handles.
   Pointer becomes a ✛.

3. Drag outline to desired location.

4. Click anywhere outside of line to deselect line.

121

GRAPHICS LINE (continued)

Size Line with Mouse

1. Click on line to size.
   A dashed border with handles (small squares) appears around line.
2. Point to a line handle.
   Pointer becomes a ⤢ ⇳ ⟷.

   NOTE: *Handles on corners of line can be used to change the line's size and thickness.*
3. Drag outline to increase or decrease line size or thickness.
4. Click anywhere outside of line to deselect line.

Edit Line

1. • Point to line to edit.
   Pointer becomes a ⇖.

   • Double-click on line.

   • Go to step 2.

OR

1. • If necessary, turn Reveal Codes on ...... **Alt**+**F3**

   • Place highlight immediately to the right of line code to edit.

   • Select Graphics menu .... **Alt**+**G**

   • Select Line .... **L**

   • Select Edit Horizontal .... **O**

     OR   **OR**

     Select Edit Vertical .... **E**

2. Select options as desired.
   See Create Horizontal Line options below step 4 on page 118.
   See Create Vertical Line options below step 4 on page 119.
3. Select OK .... **↵**

122

HARD SPACE

A special space character that keeps two words together on a line.
If the second word does not fit on a line, both words will wrap to next
line or page.

1. Place insertion point where hard space will be inserted.
2. If necessary, delete existing space . . . . `Del`
3. Select Layout menu . . . . `Alt`+`L`
4. Select Line . . . . `L`
5. Select Special Codes . . . . `O`
6. Select ◯Hard Space [HdSpc] . . . . `Alt`+`P`
7. Select Insert . . . . `⏎`

HEADERS AND FOOTERS

Repeats text on the top or bottom of pages in a document. To see your
headers or footers you must preview (page 188) or print (page 184) the
document. You can create up to two headers and footers per page.

Create Header or Footer

1. Place insertion point at top of page where header or footer
   will begin.
2. Select Layout menu . . . . `Alt`+`L`
3. Select Page . . . . `P`
4. Select Headers . . . . `H`
   OR   **OR**
   Select Footers . . . . `F`
5. Select ◯Header/Footer **A** . . . . `A`
   OR   **OR**
   Select ◯Header/Footer **B** . . . . `B`
6. Select Create . . . . `C`
7. Type and format header or footer text as desired.

Continued ...

HEADERS AND FOOTERS — Create Header or Footer (continued)

8. Select **P**lacement . . . . **Alt** + **P**

9. Select desired placement . . . . **letter**
   Every Page, Odd Pages, Even Pages

10. Select **OK** to return to header or footer window . . . . **⏎**

    To insert page number code in header or footer text:

    a) Place insertion point as desired.

    b) Select Page **N**umber . . . . **Alt** + **N**
       A ^B code appears where page number will print.

11. Select **C**lose . . . . **Alt** + **C**

Edit Header or Footer

1. If necessary, turn Reveal Codes on . . . . **Alt** + **F3**

2. Place highlight to the right of header or footer code to edit.
   NOTE: WordPerfect searches backward through document to find headers and footers.

3. Select **L**ayout menu . . . . **Alt** + **L**

4. Select **P**age . . . . **P**

5. Select **H**eaders . . . . **H**

   OR   **OR**

   Select **F**ooters . . . . **F**

6. Select ○ Header/Footer **A** . . . . **A**

   OR   **OR**

   Select ○ Header/Footer **B** . . . . **B**

7. Select **E**dit . . . . **E**

8. Type, edit, format or retrieve text as desired.

   To change placement of header or footer:

   a) Select **P**lacement . . . . **Alt** + **P**

   b) Select desired placement . . . . **letter**
      Every Page, Odd Pages, Even Pages

   c) Select **OK** to return to header or footer window . . . **⏎**

Continued ...

124

To insert page number code in header or footer text:

a) Place insertion point as desired.

b) Select Page **N**umber .... **Alt**+**N**

   A ^B code appears where page number will print.

9. Select **C**lose .... **Alt**+**C**

Discontinue Header or Footer

*Discontinues header or footer from a specific page to the end
of document.*

1. If necessary, turn Reveal Codes on .... **Alt**+**F3**

2. Place highlight to the right of header or footer code
   to discontinue.

   *NOTE: WordPerfect searches backward through document to
   find headers and footers.*

3. Select **L**ayout menu .... **Alt**+**L**

4. Select **P**age .... **P**

5. Select **H**eaders .... **H**

   OR   **OR**

   Select **F**ooters .... **F**

6. Select ○ Header/Footer **A** .... **A**

   OR   **OR**

   Select ○ Header/Footer **B** .... **B**

7. Select **D**iscontinue .... **D**

Delete Discontinued Header or Footer Code

*Use these steps when you want a header or footer that has been
discontinued (see above) to take affect again.*

• Delete [... Discontinue] code
  (see DELETE CODES on page 23).

HEADERS AND FOOTERS (continued)

Suppress Header or Footer on Current Page

1. Place insertion point at top of page where header or footer will be suppressed.

2. Select **L**ayout menu . . . . **Alt** + **L**

3. Select **P**age . . . . **P**

4. Select S**u**ppress . . . . **U**

5. Select desired header(s) or footer(s) to suppress . . . . **letter**
   *H*eader A, H*e*ader B, *F*ooter A, F*o*oter B

6. Select **OK** . . . . **⏎**

Delete Header or Footer

• Delete [Header...] or [Footer...] code
  (see DELETE CODES on page 23).

HYPHENATION

When hyphenation is turned on, Wordperfect will scan your document and hyphenate words. WordPerfect hyphenates words based on the current hyphenation zone setting (below) and the dictionary it uses. If WordPerfect cannot find a word in its dictionary, and you have set WordPerfect to prompt for hyphenation (page 128), a Position Hyphen dialog box will appear (page 127), from which you can make decisions about the word.

Turn Hyphenation On/Off

1. Place insertion point where hyphenation will begin or end.

2. Select **L**ayout menu . . . . `Alt`+`L`

3. Select **L**ine . . . . `L`

4. Select Hyph**e**nation . . . . `E`

5. Select or clear ☐**H**yphenation On . . . . `Alt`+`H`

6. Select **OK** . . . . `↵`

Set Hyphenation Zone

Expands or reduces the zone (area to the left and right of right margin) that a word must occupy before WordPerfect will hyphenate it.

1. Place insertion point where setting will begin.

2. Select **L**ayout menu . . . . `Alt`+`L`

3. Select **L**ine . . . . `L`

4. Select Hyph**e**nation . . . . `E`

5. Type a percentage in
   Percent **L**eft text box . . . . **number**

6. Select Percent **R**ight text box . . . . `Alt`+`R`

7. Type a percentage . . . . **number**

NOTE: To hyphenate more words, decrease the percentages in each text box. These numbers represent a percentage of the line length to the left or right of the right margin

8. Select **OK** . . . . `↵`

HYPHENATION (continued)

Position Hyphen Dialog Box

FROM POSITION HYPHEN DIALOG BOX

WordPerfect displays the word requiring hyphenation with a suggested hyphen position.

1. Select desired hyphen position in word . . . . 🔁

   NOTE: *WordPerfect limits hyphen position by the hyphenation zone (page 126).*

2. Select desired option:

   * Insert **H**yphen . . . . **Alt** + **H**
     to insert a soft hyphen at selected position.

     NOTE: *A <u>Soft Hyphen</u> divides a word with a hyphen where the word crosses the right margin.*

   * Hyphenation S**R**t . . . . **Alt** + **R**
     to insert a Hyphenation Soft Return and split word at selected position without a hyphen.

     NOTE: *A Hyphenation Soft Return divides a word with a space instead of a hyphen where the word crosses the right margin.*

   * Insert S**p**ace . . . . **Alt** + **P**
     to insert a space instead of a hyphen.

   * **I**gnore Word . . . . **Alt** + **I**
     to wrap the entire word to the next line.

     NOTE: *WordPerfect inserts [Hyph Ign Wrd] code to prevent word from restarting hyphenation process.*

   * **S**top Hyphenation . . . . **Alt** + **S**

3. Repeat steps for each word to hyphenate.

128

Set Hyphenation Preferences

1. Select **F**ile menu .... `Alt` + `F`
2. Select P**r**eferences .... `E`
3. Select **E**nvironment .... `E`

   To set hyphenation beep:

   - Select or clear ☐**H**yphenation
     in Beep On group .... `H`

   To set prompt for hyphenation:

   - Select desired option from Prompt for
     Hyphenation group:

     ○ **N**ever .... `N`
     sets WordPerfect to hyphenate words automatically,
     according to dictionary selected.
     NOTE: *If word is not found in dictionary,*
     entire word will wrap to next line.

     ○ **W**hen Required .... `W`
     sets WordPerfect to hyphenate words according
     to its dictionary. If word is not found in
     dictionary, the Position Hyphen Dialog
     Box (page 127) will appear.

     ○ **A**lways .... `A`
     sets WordPerfect to stop at each word
     that requires hyphenation and prompt for
     position of hyphen (see page 127).

   To specify location of hyphenation dictionary:

   - Select desired option in Hyphenation group:

     ○ E**x**ternal .... `X`

     ○ **I**nternal .... `I`
4. Select **OK** .... `↵`

HYPHENATION (continued)

Insert a Regular Hyphen

- Press – (minus key) .... ⬛️

Insert Special Hyphenation Codes

1. Place insertion point where code will be inserted.
2. Select Layout menu .... Alt + L
3. Select Line L
4. Select Special Codes .... O
5. Select desired option in Hyphenation Codes group:

   ○ Dash Character .... A
   inserts a hyphen and prevents two words
   from being separated by a soft return.
   Example: co-owner

   ○ Soft Hyphen- .... S
   divides a word at a specific location <u>with</u>
   <u>a visible hyphen</u> only when word crosses the
   right margin.

   ○ Hyphenation Soft Return [HyphSRt] .... F
   divides a word <u>with a space</u> instead of a
   hyphen only when word crosses the right margin.

6. Select Insert .... ⏎

Cancel Hyphenation on a Word

Prevents hyphenation of word, or retains a word's existing hyphenation.

1. Place insertion point on first letter of word.
2. Select Layout menu .... Alt + L
3. Select Line L
4. Select Special Codes .... O
5. Select ○ Hyphenation Ignore Word [HyphIgnWrd] .... W
6. Select Insert .... ⏎
7. If necessary, delete existing hyphen in word.

130

INDENT

Indents a paragraph without affecting margin settings for current document. A paragraph is defined as a body of text that ends with a single hard return.

1. Place insertion point where indent will begin.

2. Select Layout menu .... Alt + L

3. Select Paragraph .... R

4. Select desired indent type:

   • Indent I
     to indent left side of paragraph on next tab stop.
     NOTE: *To quickly insert an indent, from document press **F7** (CUA) or press **F4** (DOS).*

   • Double Indent .... D
     to indent left and right side of paragraph one tab stop.
     NOTE: *To quickly insert an double indent, from document press **Ctrl + Shift + F7** (CUA) or press **Shift + F4** (DOS).*

   • Hanging Indent .... H
     to indent all lines except the first line on next tab stop.

   • Margin Release .... M
     to align only the first line of text with previous tab stop (usually to the left of left margin).
     NOTE: *To quickly insert a margin release code, press **Shift + Tab** (in a document) or press **Ctrl + Shift + Tab** (in a table).*

5. If desired, type text .... **text**

   • Enter .... ⏎
     to end paragraph.

INDEX

Creating an index involves three basic steps:

• *Create a concordance file (page 131) and/or mark items to include in index (page 131).*

• *Define the index style and location (page 132).*

• *Generate the index (page 90).*

INDEX (continued)

Create Concordance File

A concordance file is a special file in which you list items that WordPerfect will use when it generates an index. When you generate an index, WordPerfect searches your document for entries in the concordance file and inserts the entry and its page number in the index.

1. Open a new document (page 161).
2. Type entry for index.
3. **Enter** . . . . ↵
4. Repeat steps 2 and 3 for each entry to add.
5. Select **T**ools menu . . . . **Alt**+**T**
6. Select So**r**t . . . . **R**
7. Select **OK** to sort document alphabetically . . . . ↵
8. Save and name concordance file (page 212).

Mark Items to Include in Index

1. Open document (page 167) containing data to index.
2. Select word or phrase (page 218) to include in index.
3. Select **T**ools menu . . . . **Alt**+**T**
4. Select Mar**k** Text . . . . **K**
5. Select **I**ndex . . . . **I**
   *Selected text appears in the **H**eading text box.*
   To use selected text as heading in index:
   - Select **OK** . . . . ↵
   To use selected text as a subheading:
   a) Type heading text in **H**eading text box . . . . **text**
   b) Select **S**ubheading text box . . . . **Tab**
      *Selected text now appears in **S**ubheading text box.*
   c) If desired, edit subheading.
   d) Select **OK** . . . . ↵
6. Repeat steps 2-5 for each item to mark.

132

Define Index Style and Location

Defines location and numbering style of index. You must execute these steps before you can generate (page 90) your index.

1. Place insertion point where index will begin.

2. Select **T**ools menu . . . . `Alt` + `T`

3. Select De**f**ine . . . . `F`

4. Select **I**ndex . . . . `I`

5. Open Numbering **F**ormat `[      ▼]` . . . . . . `Alt` + `F` , `F4`
   and select desired number format:

   - **N**o Numbering . . . . `N`

   - Text **#** — Page numbers follow entries . . . . `#`

   - **T**ext (#) — (Page numbers) follow entries . . . . `T`

   - T**e**xt   # — Flush right page numbers . . . . `E`

   - Te**x**t .....# — Flush right page numbers
     preceded by dot leaders . . . . `X`

     NOTE: *To change page numbering type (from Arabic to Roman), see Page Numbering Style on page 174.*

   ### If a concordance file was created,

   a) Select Optional **C**oncordance File text box . . . `Alt` + `C`

   b) Type concordance filename . . . . **filename**
      OR   **OR**

      Open Optional **C**oncordance File `⊟` . . . . `F4`
      and select filename (pages 25, 26).

6. Select **OK** . . . . `↵`

133

Generate Index

See GENERATE on page 90.

INITIAL CODES

Preferences Initial Codes

Sets default preferences (such as fonts, margins, tab settings)
for subsequently created documents.

1. Select File menu . . . . Alt + F
2. Select Preferences . . . . E
3. Select Initial Codes I
   The Default Initial Codes window appears.
4. Insert codes (such as margins and tab settings) as desired.
5. Select Close . . . . Alt + C

NOTE: These setting will not take effect until you open a new document.

Document's Initial Codes

Sets default preferences for current document only.

1. Select Layout menu . . . . Alt + L
2. Select Document . . . . D
3. Select Initial Codes C
   Preferences initial codes (see above), if any, are displayed
   in Document Initial Codes window.
4. Insert or delete codes (such as margins and tab settings)
   as desired.
5. Select Close to close window . . . . Alt + C

INSERTION POINT MOVEMENT (CUA)

One character left or right	`←→`
One line up or down	`↑↓`
Previous word	`Ctrl` + `←`
Next word	`Ctrl` + `→`
Top of previous page	`Alt` + `PgUp`
Top of next page	`Alt` + `PgDn`
Top of screen	`PgUp`
End of screen	`PgDn`
Top of document	`Ctrl` + `Home`
Top of document (before all codes) `Ctrl` + `Home`, `Ctrl` + `Home`	
End of document	`Ctrl` + `End`
Beginning of line	`Home`
Beginning of line (before all codes)	`Home`, `Home`
End of line	`End`
One paragraph up or down	`Ctrl` + `↑↓`

Also see GO TO on page 91.

JUSTIFICATION

Aligns all text that follows the justification code until another justification code changes the alignment. By default, WordPerfect applies left justification to your text.

Change Justification to Left, Right, Center, or Full

1. Place insertion point where justification will begin.
2. Select Layout menu .... `Alt`+`L`
3. Select Justification .... `J`
4. Select desired justification method:
   - Left — aligns text at left margin .... `L`
   - Right — aligns text at right margin .... `R`
   - Center — centers text between margins .... `C`
   - Full — forces lines of text to fill space between margins .... `F`

KERN TEXT

Kerning is an adjustment of the space between specific pairs of letters. If your printer does not support kerning, you can use ADVANCE (page 1) to kern text.

Manually Kern Text

Adjusts space between a specified pair of letters.

1. Place insertion point between letters to kern.
2. Select Layout menu .... `Alt`+`L`
3. Select Typesetting .... `N`
4. Select Manual Kerning .... `Alt`+`K`
5. Open Units ⬚ ⬍ .... `Alt`+`U`, `F4`
   and select desired unit .... **character**
   Inches, Centimeters, Points, 1200ths
6. Select Amount increment box .... `Alt`+`A`

Continued ...

136

7. Type distance between letters . . . . **number**

   > *NOTE:* *A negative number decreases space between letters.*
   > *A positive number increases space between letters.*

8. Select **OK** . . . . ↵

9. Select **OK** to return to document . . . . ↵

Set Automatic Kerning of Text On/Off

Automatic Kerning reduces space between predefined letter pairs
throughout a document or for selected text.

1. Place insertion point where kerning will begin or end.

   OR

   Select text (page 218) to kern.

2. Select Layout menu . . . . **Alt**+**L**

3. Select Typesetting . . . . **N**

4. Select or clear ☐Automatic Kerning . . . . **U**

5. Select **OK** . . . . ↵

KEYBOARD LAYOUT

Select a Keyboard Layout

1. Select File menu . . . . **Alt**+**F**

2. Select Preferences . . . . **E**

3. Select Keyboard . . . . **K**

4. Select Select . . . . **S**

5. Type filename of keyboard in
   Filename text box . . . . **filename**

   OR   **OR**

   Select desired keyboard file from
   Files list box . . . . **Alt**+**I**, ↕

6. Select Select . . . . ↵

7. Select **OK** . . . . ↵

137

Create a Keyboard Layout

Assigns commands, macros, text or menu options to keystrokes.

1. Select File menu .... `Alt`+`F`
2. Select Preferences .... `E`
3. Select Keyboard .... `K`
4. Select Create .... `R`
5. Press keystroke to which an item will be assigned.

   Example: Ctrl + 1

   NOTE: If selected keystroke is already assigned to an item, the name and type of item are displayed on current text line in Change Assignment group box. Otherwise, "Unassigned" is displayed.

6. Open Item Types `[    ⧨]` .... `Alt`+`I`, `Space` and select desired item:

   - Commands .... `C`
     lists commands that can be assigned to a keystroke.
   - Menus .... `M`
     lists menu items that can be assigned to a keystroke.
   - Text .... `T`
     lists text items that can be assigned to a keystroke.

   If desired text item is not listed,

   a) Select Add .... `Alt`+`D`
   b) Type a name for text in Name text box ..... **name**
   c) Select Text text box .... `Alt`+`T`
   d) Type text .... **text**

   OR   **OR**

   Press **Shift + Ins** (Paste) .... `Shift`+`Ins` to paste Clipboard contents to text box.

   NOTE: Press Ctrl + Enter to break lines in text.

   e) Select OK .... `↵`

   NOTE: To edit a text item, select item, then select Edit.

Continued ...

138

KEYBOARD LAYOUT (continued)

- **Macros** .... `A`
  lists macros that can be assigned to a keystroke.
  If desired macro is not listed,
  - a) Select A**d**d .... `Alt`+`D`
  - b) Select macro filename
    in **F**iles list box .... `Alt`+`I`, `↑⁄₄`
  - c) Select **I**mport .... `↵`

    NOTE: *A "Macro needs to be compiled first" message*
    appears if you have not run the selected macro
    (see Play Back a Macro on page 150).

7. Select item to which keystroke will be
   assigned in Assignable Items list box ...... `Tab`, `↑⁄₄`

8. Select **A**ssign .... `Alt`+`A`

   If a menu item was selected and you want
   keystroke displayed on a pull-down menu,
   - a) Select keystroke to display in
     Current **K**eystrokes list .... `Alt`+`K`, `↑⁄₄`
   - b) Select ☐ Display as
     Shortcut Keystroke on **M**enu .... `Alt`+`M`

9. Repeat steps 5-8 for each keystroke to assign.

10. Select **S**ave As .... `Alt`+`S`

11. Type filename for keyboard layout
    in Save **A**s text box .... **filename**
    NOTE: *Filename must have a "WWK" extension.*

12. Select **S**ave .... `↵`

13. Select **OK** .... `↵`

14. Select **OK** to return to document .... `Tab`, `↵`
    *Press **Tab** until OK is outlined.*

Edit Keyboard Layout or Update WP 5.1 Keyboard

1. Select File menu . . . . `Alt` + `F`
2. Select Preferences . . . . `E`
3. Select Keyboard . . . . `K`
4. Select Select . . . . `S`
5. Select keyboard file in Files list box . . . `Alt` + `I`, `↹`
6. Select Select . . . . `↵`
7. Select Edit . . . . `E`

   To update WP 5.1 keyboard for use with WP 5.2:

   a) Select Save As . . . . `Alt` + `S`
   b) Select Save . . . . `Alt` + `S`
   c) Select OK to overwrite file . . . . `↵`

8. If editing keyboard, assign keystrokes as desired.
   See steps 5-9 on pages 137 and 138.
9. Select OK . . . . `↵`
10. Select OK to return to document . . . . `Tab`, `↵`
    Press Tab until OK is outlined.

LABELS

When you create a label page definition, it is assigned to the current printer driver. A printer driver is a program file that controls a printer.

Create or Edit a Label Paper Type

1. Select printer (page 194) for which label paper type will be created.
2. If using label now, place insertion point at top of page where label definition will begin.

   NOTE: *If editing a label setting that is in the document, press Alt + F3 (Reveal Codes) and place highlight immediately to the right of the code.*

3. Select Layout menu . . . . `Alt` + `L`

Continued ...

140

4. Select **P**age . . . . `P`

5. Select Paper **S**ize . . . . `S`

6. Select **A**dd . . . . `Alt`+`A`
   to create a new label definition.

   OR   **OR**

   Select label to edit . . . . `↑⁄↓`

   • Select **E**dit . . . . `Alt`+`E`

If using WPWIN 5.1 with a <u>Windows printer driver</u>,

> *NOTE:* *If <u>creating</u> a label, WordPerfect displays a message.*
> *Read message then select OK.*

FROM EDIT LABELS DIALOG BOX

   a) Select desired label field . . . . `Tab`

   b) Type appropriate number . . . . **number**

   c) Repeat steps b and c for each field to change.

   d) Select **OK** . . . . `↵`

If using WPWIN 5.2 or WPWIN 5.1 with a WP printer driver,

FROM ADD/EDIT PAPER SIZE DIALOG BOX

   a) If desired, change options in Add Paper Size dialog box.
      (See Create a Paper Definition options below step 5 on page 177.)

   b) Open Paper **T**ype `[      ⬍]` . . . . `Alt`+`T`, `F4`

      <u>and</u> select **L**abels . . . . `L`

   c) Select **L**abels . . . . `Alt`+`L`

FROM EDIT LABELS DIALOG BOX

   d) Select desired label field . . . . `Tab`

   e) Type appropriate number . . . . **number**

   f) Repeat steps d and e for each field to change.

   g) Select **OK** twice . . . . `↵`, `↵`

7. To use label now, select **S**elect . . . . `Alt`+`S`

   OR   **OR**

   Select **Close** . . . . `Alt`+`F4`

LABELS (continued)

Select a Label Paper Type
See Select an Existing Paper Definition on page 176.

Delete a Label Paper Type
See Delete or Copy a Paper Definition on page 180.

LANGUAGE

Specifies language of text in a document. Language code determines which dictionary, thesaurus, and hyphenation files WordPerfect uses, how dates are formatted, how words in dates are spelled, and what order WordPerfect uses for sorting.

Change Language Code

1. Place insertion point where new language will be inserted.

   OR

   Select text (page 218) for which language will be changed.

2. Select Tools menu . . . . `Alt`+`T`

3. Select Language . . . . `L`

4. Select desired language from
   Current Language list box . . . . `↑/↓`

   NOTE: *The Current Language list box lists all languages WordPerfect currently supports or will support in the future.*

5. Select OK . . . . `↵`

LINE DRAW

Provides tools for drawing straight lines and boxes with preset characters or characters from the WordPerfect Character Set.

1. Place insertion point where drawing will begin.

2. Select a fixed-pitch font (see Change Base Font on page 84).

3. Select **T**ools menu . . . . `Alt`+`T`

4. Select L**i**ne Draw . . . . `I`
   Starts draft mode and displays a Line Draw dialog box.

5. Select desired character in Characters group . . . . . . `Tab`
   *Press **Tab** until desired character is selected.*

   OR   **OR**

   Select **C**haracter . . . . `Alt`+`C`

   a) Type a character . . . . **character**

      OR   **OR**

      Press **Ctrl + W** (WordPerfect Character) . . . `Ctrl`+`W`

      • Select desired character (page 275).

   b) Select **OK** . . . . `↵`

   To switch between drawing modes:

   • Select one of the following:

      ○ **D**raw . . . . `Alt`+`D`

      ○ **M**ove . . . . `Alt`+`M`

      ○ **E**rase . . . . `Alt`+`E`

6. Press **arrow** keys in direction
   to move, draw, or erase . . . . `⇅`

   To remove arrow from end of line:

   a) If necessary, move to end of line.

   b) Press **Alt + End** . . . . `Alt`+`End`

Continued ...

LINE DRAW (continued)

To draw lines quickly:

- Extend line to any margin or next line ..... `Ctrl`+`↕`

- Extend line to left margin
and through existing lines .... `Home`

- Extend line to right margin
and through existing lines .... `End`

7. To end Line Draw, select **Close** .... `↵`

LINE HEIGHT

Determines space between the baseline of one line and the baseline of the next line in single-spaced text.

1. Place insertion point where new line height will begin.

   OR

   Select text (page 218) to change.

2. Select **L**ayout menu .... `Alt`+`L`

3. Select **L**ine .... `L`

4. Select **H**eight .... `H`

5. Select ○ **A**uto .... `A`

   OR   **OR**

   Select ○ **F**ixed .... `F`

   a) Select text box .... `Tab`

   b) Type new line height (inches) .... **number**

6. Select **OK** .... `↵`

   NOTE: *If you have selected First Baseline at Top Margin in the Typesetting dialog box (page 271), you must use a fixed line height.*

144

LINE HEIGHT (LEADING) ADJUSTMENT

Adjusts vertical space between lines of text in a paragraph (lines separated by soft return codes) and vertical space between paragraphs (text separated by hard returns).

1. Place insertion point where line height change will begin.

   OR

   Select text (page 218) to change.

2. Select **L**ayout menu . . . . **Alt** + **L**

3. Select Typesetti**n**g . . . . **N**

4. Select Between **L**ines: [SRt] text box . . . . **Alt** + **L**

5. Type distance (inches) . . . . **number**

   NOTE: *A negative number decreases vertical space between lines; a positive number increases this space.*

6. Select Between P**a**ragraphs: [HRt] text box . . . . . **Alt** + **A**

7. Type distance (inches) . . . . **number**

   NOTE: *A negative number decreases vertical space between paragraphs; a positive number increases this space.*

8. Select **OK** . . . . **↵**

LINE NUMBERING

Numbers lines in a document and prints number of each line at a specified position on a page. You must print (page 184) or preview (page 188) the document to see numbers.

1. Place insertion point where line numbering will begin or end.

2. Select **L**ayout menu . . . . **Alt** + **L**

3. Select **L**ine . . . . **L**

4. Select **N**umbering . . . . **N**

5. Open **L**ine Numbering [⬚ ▼] . . . . **Alt** + **L**, **F4**

   a**n**d select desired option . . . . **letter**

   O̲ff, R̲estart Each Page, C̲ontinuous

Continued ...

LINE NUMBERING (continued)

To change position of numbers:

a) Select <u>P</u>osition from Left Edge text box . . . . . `Alt`+`P`

b) Type distance (inches) . . . . **number**

To change starting number:

a) Select <u>S</u>tarting Number text box . . . . `Alt`+`S`

b) Type new line number . . . . **number**

To indicate lines to number:

a) Select <u>N</u>umber Every text box . . . . `Alt`+`N`

b) Type interval . . . . **number**
    Example: 5 (will number every five lines, 5, 10, 15, etc.)

To count blank lines:

Select or clear ☐<u>C</u>ount Blank Lines . . . . `Alt`+`C`

6. Select **OK** . . . . `↵`

LINE SPACING

1. Place insertion point where line spacing change will begin.

    OR

    Select text (page 218) to change.

2. Select <u>L</u>ayout menu . . . . `Alt`+`L`

3. Select <u>L</u>ine . . . . `L`

4. Select <u>S</u>pacing . . . . `S`

5. Type new spacing (inches) in increment box . . . . . **number**

6. Select **OK** . . . . `↵`

LIST

Creates list of tables, figures, illustrations, maps, or any item you mark within a document.

NOTE: *You can create up to ten lists within a document. When you generate a list, WordPerfect lists the entries in the same order they appear in the document.*

There are three basics steps for creating a list:

- *If making a list of text, mark text (see below) to include in list.*
- *Define location and numbering style of list (see below).*
- *Generate list (page 90).*

Mark Text for List

NOTE: *These steps are not required when creating preassigned lists (Lists 6-10) for captions contained in graphics boxes.*

1. Select word or phrase (page 218) to include in list.
2. Select **T**ools menu .... `Alt`+`T`
3. Select Mar**k** Text .... `K`
4. Select **L**ist .... `L`
5. Open Number `[    ◆]` .... `F4`

   <u>and</u> select desired list .... **number**

   List 1, List 2, List 3, List 4, List 5
6. Select **OK** .... `↵`
7. Repeat steps 1-6 for each item to mark.

Define List Type, Style and Location

1. Place insertion point on page where list will appear.
2. Select **T**ools menu .... `Alt`+`T`
3. Select De**f**ine .... `F`
4. Select **L**ist .... `L`
5. Open **L**ist `[    ◆]` .... `Alt`+`L`, `F4`

   <u>and</u> select desired list .... **number**

   List 1, List 2, List 3, List 4, List 5, List 6 (Figure Captions),
   List 7 (Table Captions), List 8 (Text Box Captions),
   List 9 (User Box Captions), List 10 (Equation Captions)

Continued ...

LIST — Define List Type, Style and Location (continued)

6. Open Numbering Format [⬍] . . . . . . `Alt`+`F`, `F4`
   <u>and</u> select desired number style:

   - <u>N</u>o numbering . . . . `N`
   - Text <u>#</u> — Page numbers follows entries . . . . `#`
   - <u>T</u>ext (#) — (Page numbers) follows entries . . . . `T`
   - T<u>e</u>xt   # — Flush right page numbers . . . . `E`
   - Te<u>x</u>t....# — Flush right page numbers
     preceded by dot leaders . . . . `X`

   NOTE: *To change page numbering type (from Arabic*
   to Roman), see Page Numbering on page 174.

7. Select **OK** . . . . `↵`
8. Repeat steps 1-7 for each list to define.

Generate List

See GENERATE on page 90.

LOCATION OF FILES (Preferences)

Determines location of WordPerfect files including: spelling, thesaurus, and hyphenation dictionaries, as well as backup, documents, graphics, printer, spreadsheet, keyboard, button bar, macro, and style files.

1. Select File menu .... `Alt` + `F`
2. Select Preferences .... `E`
3. Select Location of Files .... `L`

   To set default location of files:

   a) Select desired file category text box ..... `Alt` + **letter**
      Backup Files, Documents, Graphics Files, Printer Files, Spreadsheets, Files — for macros, keyboards and button bars, Directory — for styles, Main dictionary, Supplementary dictionary

   b) Type drive and directory .... **path**
      Example: c:\wpwin\graphics
      OR   **OR**
      Open `B` for selected category .... `F4`
      and select directory location (pages 25, 26).

   c) Repeat steps a and b for each file category to change.

   To set default style:

   a) Select Filename text box .... `Alt` + `F`

   b) Type location and filename of style .... **path\filename**
      Example: C:\wpwin\library.sty
      OR   **OR**
      Open Filename `B` .... `F4`
      and select filename of style (pages 25, 26).

4. Select OK .... `↵`

MACRO

Macros are recorded commands or keystrokes that can be played back to dramatically speed up the time it takes to perform a task.

Record a Macro

NOTE: You can record a macro from WordPerfect or from the Macro Facility, but it's easier to record a macro from WordPerfect.

1. Select Macro menu .... **Alt** + **M**

2. Select Record .... **R**

3. Type filename for macro in Filename text box .. **filename**

   NOTE: Do not type a filename extension (WordPerfect adds .WCM to filename). Unless you indicate a drive and directory, WordPerfect saves macro to location specified in Location of Files (page 148) dialog box.

OR   **OR**

Press **Ctrl** + key (*WP5.2*) .... **Ctrl** +key
to name and assign macro to a keystroke.

   *NOTE: "key" can be a letter or number, or "key" can be **Shift** + letter or number.*

Examples: Ctrl + 1 or Ctrl + Shift + a

To add descriptive name to macro:

a) Select Descriptive Name text box .... **Alt** + **D**

b) Type descriptive name .... **text**

To add summary notes about macro:

a) Select Abstract text box .... **Alt** + **A**

b) Type notes .... **text**

   *NOTE: Press **Ctrl** + **Enter** to insert a line break.*

4. Select Record .... **⏎**

If recording from Macro Facility,

   • Select WordPerfect application window.

The "Recording Macro" message appears in status bar until recording of macro is completed.

Continued ...

150

MACRO — Record a Macro (continued)

5. Type text or execute commands to record.

   NOTE: *The mouse cannot be used to position insertion point.*

   To pause/resume recording of macro:

   a) Select **M**acro menu .... `Alt`+`M`

   b) Select or deselect Pa**u**se .... `U`
   to pause or resume recording.

6. Select **M**acro menu .... `Alt`+`M`

7. Select **S**top to end recording of macro .... `S`

Play Back a Macro

- Place insertion point where macro will execute.

   To play back a macro assigned to a keystroke:

   - Press keystroke.

   To play back a macro assigned to the Button Bar:

   - Click on desired button on button bar.

   To play back a macro assigned to the Macro menu:

   a) Select **M**acro menu .... `Alt`+`M`

   b) Select number of desired macro .... **number**

   To play back a macro using Play command:

   a) Select **M**acro menu .... `Alt`+`M`

   b) Select **P**lay .... `P`

   c) Type macro filename in **F**ilename text box .. **filename**

   OR   **OR**

   Select macro filename in F**i**les list box `Alt`+`I`, `↕`

   d) Select **P**lay .... `↵`

   To Stop Playback of a Macro:

   - Press **Esc** .... `Esc`

NOTE: *The first time you run a new or edited macro, WordPerfect compiles the macro.*

MACRO (continued)

Add or Edit a Macro in Macro Menu

NOTE: Up to nine macros can be assigned to the Macro menu.

1. Select **M**acro menu .... `Alt`+`M`
2. Select **A**ssign to Menu .... `A`
3. Select **I**nsert to add a macro .... `Alt`+`I`

   OR   **OR**

   Select macro to edit in Menu **T**ext list box .... `↑↓`

   • Select **E**dit .... `Alt`+`E`

   To add or change macro filename:

   • Type a macro filename
     in Macro **N**ame text box .... **filename**

     OR   **OR**

     Open Macro **N**ame `▤` .... `F4`
     and select macro filename (pages 25, 26).

   To add or change macro menu text:

   a) Select Menu **T**ext text box .... `Tab`
   b) Type or edit text .... **text**

4. Select **OK** .... `↵`
5. Select **OK** to return to document .... `Tab`, `↵`
   Press Tab until OK is outlined.

Remove a Macro from Macro Menu

1. Select **M**acro menu .... `Alt`+`M`
2. Select **A**ssign to Menu .... `A`
3. Select macro to remove in Menu **T**ext list box ..... `↑↓`
4. Select **D**elete .... `Alt`+`D`
5. Repeat steps 3 and 4 for each macro to delete.
6. Select **OK** .... `↵`

NOTE: When you remove a macro from the menu, its file is not deleted and the macro can still be used.

152

MACRO (continued)

Compile a Macro

A macro must be compiled before it can be nested in another macro or before it can be assigned to a keystroke.

1. Run or select Macro Facility (page 153).

2. Select **M**acro menu from Macro Facility ..... **Alt** + **M**

3. Select **C**ompile Macro .... **C**

4. Type macro filename in **F**ilename text box .... **filename**

   OR   **OR**

   Select desired macro filename
   in **F**iles list box .... **Alt** + **I** , **¼**
   (See DIRECTORIES — LOCATING FILES on page 25.)

5. Select **C**ompile .... **Alt** + **C**

6. Select **OK** when macro is compiled .... **↵**

7. Select **Cancel** to exit dialog box .... **Alt** + **F4**

Convert WP 5.1.1 DOS Macros

1. Run or select Macro Facility (page 153).

2. Select **M**acro menu from Macro Facility ..... **Alt** + **M**

3. Select Con**v**ert .... **V**

4. Type macro filename in **F**ilename text box .... **filename**

   OR   **OR**

   Select desired macro filename
   in **F**iles list box .... **Alt** + **I** , **¼**
   (See DIRECTORIES — LOCATING FILES on page 25.)

5. Select **C**onvert .... **Alt** + **C**

   NOTE: A message is displayed when the conversion is completed. The converted macro will have the same name as the old macro with the exception of the file extension which will be .WCM.

6. Select **OK** when conversion is completed .... **↵**

7. Select **Cancel** to exit dialog box .... **Alt** + **F4**

MACRO (continued)

Run or Select Macro Facility

When you play back a macro, the Macro Facility application runs automatically. You can also run the Macro Facility as a separate application from Windows Program Manager.

To run Macro Facility from Windows Program Manager:

1. Select <u>F</u>ile menu from Program Manager . . . .   **Alt** + **F**

2. Select <u>R</u>un . . . . **R**

3. Type C:\WPC\MFWIN.EXE . . . . **c:\wpc\MFWIN.EXE**

4. Select **OK** . . . . **↵**

To select Macro Facility application:

1. Press and <u>hold</u> **Alt** . . . . **Alt**

   <u>while</u> pressing and releasing **Tab** . . . . **Tab**
   until Macro Facility name is displayed or its
   title is highlighted.

2. Release keys to select.

MARGINS

Set Margins

Also see Set Left and Right Margins using the Ruler on page 208.

1. Place insertion point where new margins will begin.

   OR

   Select text (page 218) for which margins will change.

2. Select **L**ayout menu . . . . **Alt** + **L**

3. Select **M**argins . . . . **M**

4. Select text box of margin to change . . . . . . **Alt** + **letter**
   *L*eft, *T*op, *R*ight, *B*ottom

5. Type new margin position . . . . **number**
   Where zero is the left, top, right, or bottom edge of page.

6. Repeat steps 4 and 5 for each margin to change.

7. Select **OK** . . . . **↵**

MASTER DOCUMENT

Use a master document to divide a large document into manageable subdocuments. You can accomplish this by inserting links to subdocuments in the master document. These links mark the location where the subdocuments will be inserted when you expand the master document.

Insert Subdocument Link in Master Document

1. Open document that will serve as the master document.

2. Place insertion point where subdocument link will be inserted.

3. Select <u>T</u>ools menu . . . . `Alt`+`T`

4. Select M<u>a</u>ster Document . . . . `A`

5. Select <u>S</u>ubdocument . . . . `S`

6. Type subdocument's filename
   in <u>F</u>ilename text box . . . . **filename**

   OR   **OR**

   Select filename from F<u>i</u>les list box . . . . . `Alt`+`I`, `↹`
   See DIRECTORIES — LOCATING FILES, page 25.

7. Select <u>I</u>nclude . . . . `↵`
   A comment appears showing placement of link and name of subdocument.

8. Repeat steps 2-7 for each subdocument that will make up the master document.

Expand Master Document

Retrieves subdocuments text into master document.
FROM MASTER DOCUMENT

1. Select <u>T</u>ools menu . . . . `Alt`+`T`

2. Select M<u>a</u>ster Document . . . . `A`

3. Select <u>E</u>xpand Master . . . . `E`

156

Condense Master Document

Removes subdocuments text from master document. It does not remove the links.

FROM MASTER DOCUMENT

1. Select **T**ools menu .... `Alt`+`T`
2. Select M**a**ster Document .... `A`
3. Select **C**ondense Master .... `C`

FROM CONDENSE MASTER DOCUMENT DIALOG BOX
The message "Save All Subdocuments?" appears.

4. Select **N**o .... `N`
   to condense master document without saving
   changes to subdocument files.

OR   **OR**

Select **Y**es .... `Y`
to save changes to subdocument files.

If Yes was selected,

   To replace all existing subdocuments without prompting:

   • Clear ☐**P**rompt Before Replacing
     Subdocuments .... `P`

   To replace (update) existing subdocuments:

   • Select **Y**es .... `Y`

OR   **OR**

   To save subdocuments with new filenames:

   a) Select **N**o .... `N`
   b) Type new subdocument filename ...... **filename**
   c) Select **OK** .... `⏎`
   d) Repeat steps for each subdocument.

MASTER DOCUMENT (continued)

Save Master Document

1. Select File menu .... `Alt`+`F`

2. Select Save .... `S`

   OR   **OR**

   Select Save As .... `A`

   If a master document is expanded,
   The message "Document is expanded, condense it?" appears.

   a) Select No .... `N`
      to save document in its expanded form.

      OR   **OR**

      Select Yes .... `Y`
      to condense master document.

      • Follow step 4 (Condense Master Document) on
        previous page.

3. If necessary, type a filename
   in Save As text box .... filename

   • Select Save .... `↵`

MERGE

*The process of combining information in two or more documents to
create a new document. To do a merge you must:*

• *Create a primary document — the document that controls the merge.*

• *Create a secondary file — the source that contains information for the
  primary file.*

• *Execute the Merge command and supply the names of the primary
  and secondary file.*

MERGE (continued)

Create a Secondary Merge File

Contains sources that provide text and information (records) for the primary file when a merge is executed. A record contains related information grouped in fields. A field is a single element in a record.

1. Open a new document window (page 161).

2. Type data for field.

   NOTE: *If a field within a record is blank, you must still mark a position for that field in the record. There must be the same number of fields in every record.*

3. Select **T**ools menu .... **Alt** + **T**

4. Select **M**erge .... **M**

5. Select **E**nd Field .... **E**

6. Repeat steps 2-5 for each field in the record.

7. Select **T**ools menu .... **Alt** + **T**

8. Select **M**erge .... **M**

9. Select End **R**ecord .... **R**

   WordPerfect inserts a Hard Page break.

   NOTE: *Never insert blank lines between records.*

10. Repeat steps 2-9 for each record.

11. When the last record has been entered, press **Backspace** to delete page break .... **BkSp**

12. Save secondary merge file (page 212).

Example:

Without a Blank Field	With a Blank Field
Mr.{END FIELD}	Ms.{END FIELD}
Scott{END FIELD}	Monica Necole{END FIELD}
Capizzi{END FIELD}	Salazar{END FIELD}
President{END FIELD}	{END FIELD}
Magic Carpet{END FIELD}	Tri-Star Music{END FIELD}
394 Colon Ave{END FIELD}	40-70 Hampton St{END FIELD}
Staten Island{END FIELD}	Elmhurst{END FIELD}
NY{END FIELD}	NY{END FIELD}
10308{END FIELD}	11379{END FIELD}
{END RECORD}	{END RECORD)

MERGE (continued)

Create a Primary Merge File

A primary file contains merge codes that control the merge and may also contain text. For example, a form letter.

NOTE: *Each field in a record is numbered.*

> **Example:** *{FIELD}1~ = Title*
> *{FIELD}2~ = First name*

1. Open new document window (page 161).

2. As needed, type text, then place insertion point where field will be placed.

3. Select <u>T</u>ools menu . . . . **Alt** + **T**

4. Select <u>M</u>erge . . . . **M**

5. Select <u>F</u>ield . . . . **F**

6. Type number of field . . . . **number**

> **NOTE:** *WordPerfect inserts a field code with the specified number (i.e., {FIELD}1~). The field number must correspond to an existing field position of a record in a secondary merge file.*

7. Select **OK** . . . . **↵**

8. Repeat steps 2-7 for each field.

9. Save document (page 212).

Example:

Primary File	**Merged Record**
Today's Date	Today's Date
{FIELD}1~{FIELD}2~{FIELD}3~	Mr. Scott Capizzi
{FIELD}4~	President
{FIELD}5~	Magic Carpet
{FIELD}6~	394 Colon Ave
{FIELD}7~{FIELD}8~{FIELD}9~	Staten Island, NY 10308
Dear {FIELD}1~ {FIELD}3~:	Dear Mr. Capizzi:
Thank you, {FIELD}1~ {FIELD}3~,	Thank you, Mr. Capizzi,
for attending our meeting.	for attending our meeting.

MERGE (continued)

Create a Merge Document

1. Open a new document window (page 161).

2. Select **T**ools menu . . . . `Alt`+`T`

3. Select **M**erge . . . . `M`

4. Select **M**erge . . . . `M`

5. Type filename of primary file in
   Primary File text box . . . . **filename**

   OR   **OR**

   Open **P**rimary File ▣ . . . . `F4`
   and select filename (pages 25, 26).

6. Select **S**econdary File text box . . . . `Tab`

7. Type filename of secondary file . . . . **filename**

   OR   **OR**

   Open **S**econdary File ▣ . . . . `F4`
   and select filename (pages 25, 26).

8. Select **OK** . . . . `↵`
   The merged document appears in document window.

NEW DOCUMENT WINDOW

Opens a new document window. Up to nine document windows can be opened at the same time, providing your computer has enough free memory.

1. Select File menu . . . . **Alt**+**F**
2. Select New . . . . **N**

A new document window will appear in front of existing documents. Also see DOCUMENT WINDOWS on pages 35-37.

OBJECT LINKING AND EMBEDDING (OLE)

WordPerfect documents can include objects such as charts, graphics, spreadsheets, sound clips, or video files created in other Windows applications. You can embed or link objects. When you create an <u>embedded object</u>, a copy of the object is placed in your document. When you edit an embedded object, you edit the copy, not the original data. When you create a <u>linked object</u>, the object maintains a link to the source document. When you edit a linked object, you edit the original data, and all objects linked to the same data will be updated.

Embed an Object

1. Place insertion point where object will be embedded.
2. Select Edit menu . . . . **Alt**+**E**
3. Select Insert Object . . . . **I**

   The available applications that support OLE are listed in the Insert Object dialog box.

4. Select application that will create the object . . . . . . **↕**
5. Select OK . . . . **↵**
   to open application in which object will be created.

6. Create the object.

   NOTE: An object is data created in a Windows application. For example, you could create a drawing in Paintbrush or open an existing Paintbrush file.

7. Select application's File menu . . . . **Alt**+**F**
8. Select Exit and Return to *DOCUMENT NAME* . . . . . . **X**

   NOTE: Your application may show a different Exit option.

9. Select Yes to update object and insert into document . **Y**

The object appears enclosed in a figure box.

162

Edit Embedded Object

1. Double-click on object.

> **NOTE:** *In most cases, double-clicking on the object will permit editing of object in its source application. You can press the right mouse button while pointing to the object to open a QuickMenu from which you can select Edit Object, Box Position, or Edit Caption options.*

OR

Select Graphics menu . . . . `Alt`+`G`

  a) Select Figure . . . . `F`

  b) Select Edit . . . . `E`

  c) Type number of box to edit . . . . **number**

  d) Select **OK** . . . . `↵`

2. Make changes in source application.

3. Select application's File menu . . . . `Alt`+`F`

4. Select Exit and Return to *DOCUMENT NAME* . . . . `X`

> **NOTE:** *Your application may show a different Exit option.*

5. Select Yes to save file and
   update copy of object in document . . . . `↵`

Link Object

1. From a Windows application that supports object linking, create or open file that contains data to link.

2. Save the file.

3. If desired, select part of data to link.

4. Select application's Edit menu . . . . `Alt`+`E`

5. Select Copy . . . . `C`

6. Select WordPerfect application.

7. Place insertion point as desired.

8. Select Edit menu . . . . `Alt`+`E`

9. Select Paste Link . . . . `L`

The object appears enclosed in a figure box.

OBJECT LINKING AND EMBEDDING (continued)

Edit Linked Object

When you edit a linked object, the application that created the object is opened. Changes made to a linked object affect all linked objects associated with the source document.

1. Double-click on object.

   NOTE: In most cases, double-clicking on the object will permit editing of a linked object in its source application. You can press the right mouse button while pointing to the object to open a QuickMenu from which you can select Edit Object, Box Position, or Edit Caption options.

   OR

   Select Graphics menu .... `Alt`+`G`

   a) Select Figure .... `F`

   b) Select Edit .... `E`

   c) Type number of box to edit .... **number**

   d) Select OK .... `↵`

2. Make changes in source application.

   NOTE: Linked object in active WordPerfect document is updated as changes are made.

3. Save the file.

4. Select application's File menu .... `Alt`+`F`

5. Select Exit .... `X`

   NOTE: Your application may show a different Exit option.

Cancel Link to an Object

Removes link without deleting object from document.

1. Select Edit menu .... `Alt`+`E`

2. Select Links .... `K`

3. If necessary, select ○Show OLE Links ..... `Alt`+`O`

4. Select link to delete in Links list box ... `Alt`+`L`, `↕`

5. Select Cancel Link .... `Alt`+`C`

6. Select OK .... `↵`

164

Change Link

Changes the source file of an object.

1. Select Edit menu . . . . `Alt`+`E`
2. Select Links . . . . `K`
3. If necessary, select ○Show OLE Links . . . . . `Alt`+`O`
4. Select link to change in Links list box . . `Alt`+`L`, `↑↓`
5. Select Change Link . . . . `Alt`+`H`
6. Select desired filename in Files list box . `Alt`+`I`, `↑↓`
   (See DIRECTORIES — LOCATING FILES on page 25.)
   NOTE: The file you select must have been created using the process described in Link Object (page 162).
7. Select OK . . . . `↵`
8. Select OK to return to document . . . . `↵`

Update Link

Manually updates a link. Sets Update Link mode.

1. Select Edit menu . . . . `Alt`+`E`
2. Select Links . . . . `K`
3. If necessary, select ○Show OLE links . . . . . . `Alt`+`O`
4. Select link to update in Links list box . . . `Alt`+`L`, `↑↓`
5. Select Update Now . . . . `Alt`+`U`

   To change default mode for updating links:

   • Select ○Manual . . . . `Alt`+`M`

   OR   **OR**

   Select ○Automatic . . . . `Alt`+`A`
6. Select OK . . . . `↵`

OBJECT LINKING AND EMBEDDING (continued)

Paste Packaged Object

Inserts a packaged object created by the Windows Object Packager utility into a document.

1. From source application,
   - Copy data to package to the Clipboard.
     Refer to your Windows documentation.

     OR

     Create and save file to package.

2. Close the source application.

3. Run Object Packager from Program Manager ..
   Refer to your Windows documentation.

4. Paste data from Clipboard into Object Packager.

   OR

   Import a file to package.
   Refer to your Windows documentation.

5. Select **E**dit menu from Object Packager .... **Alt** + **E**

6. Select Copy Pac**k**age .... **K**

7. Select WordPerfect application.

8. Place insertion point in document where packaged object will be inserted.

9. Select **E**dit menu from WordPerfect .... **Alt** + **E**

10. Select **P**aste .... **P**
    The object appears as an icon in a figure box.

166

Activate Packaged Object

When you activate a packaged object, the contents of the package will be viewed (if a graphic), run (if a command file), or played back (if a sound or video file).

- Double-click on packaged object.

    OR

    Select Graphics menu . . . . **Alt** + **G**

    a) Select Figure . . . . **F**

    b) Select Edit . . . . **E**

    c) Type number of box to edit . . . . **number**

    d) Select OK . . . . **↵**

Edit Packaged Object

NOTE: Step one requires a mouse.

1. Click on packaged object.

    NOTE: You can press the right mouse button while pointing to the object to open a QuickMenu from which you can select Package Object, Box Position, or Edit Caption options.

2. Select Edit menu . . . . **Alt** + **E**

3. Select Package Object . . . . **O**

4. Select Edit Package . . . . **E**

5. From Object Packager, change package as desired.
    Refer to your Windows documentation.

6. Select File menu from Object Packager . . . . . **Alt** + **F**

7. Select Exit . . . . **X**

8. Select Yes (Update) . . . . **↵**

OPEN DOCUMENT WINDOW

Retrieves a file from disk into a new document window.
Also see Retrieve Document on page 206.

NOTE: *Up to nine document windows can be opened at one time, providing your computer has enough free memory.*

1. Select **F**ile menu . . . . `Alt` + `F`
2. Select **O**pen . . . . `O`
3. Type a filename in **F**ilename text box . . . . **filename**

   OR   **OR**

   Select filename in **F**iles list box . . . . . . `Alt` + `I`, `¼`

   See DIRECTORIES — LOCATING FILES, page 25.
4. Select **O**pen . . . . `↵`

OUTLINE

Create Outline

1. Place insertion point where outline will begin.
2. Select **T**ools menu . . . . `Alt` + `T`
3. Select **O**utline . . . . `O`
4. Select Outline **O**n . . . . `O`
5. **Enter** to insert first-level outline number . . . . `↵`
6. Type outline text . . . . **text**

   To insert a next outline number for current level:

   • **Enter** . . . . `↵`

     NOTE: *If there is no text on current line,*
     WordPerfect adds a blank line.

   To change to <u>next outline level</u>:

   a) Place insertion point immediately to the right
      or left of an existing outline number.

   b) Press **Tab** . . . . `Tab`
      <u>until</u> desired number for outline level appears.

Continued ...

168

OUTLINE — Create Outline (continued)

To change to <u>previous outline level</u>:

a) Place insertion point immediately to the right or left of outline number to change.

b) Press **Shift + Tab** (Margin Release) . . . `Shift` + `Tab`
<u>until</u> desired number for outline level appears.

To delete an outline number:

a) Place insertion point immediately to the right of number.

b) Press **Backspace** . . . . `BkSp`

To indent text without changing outline levels:

• Press **F7** (CUA) . . . . `F7`

OR   **OR**

Press **F4** (WP 5.1 DOS) . . . . `F4`

To move among outline levels:

• Previous outline number . . . . `Alt` + `←`

• Next outline number . . . . `Alt` + `→`

• Previous outline number in same level . . . . `Alt` + `↑`

• Next outline number in same level . . . . . . `Alt` + `↓`

Turn Outline Off

1. Place insertion point where outlining will end.

2. Select **T**ools menu . . . . `Alt` + `T`

3. Select **O**utline . . . . `O`

4. Select Outline O**f**f . . . . `F`

OUTLINE (continued)

Move or Copy Outline Family

An outline family consists of the outline level at the cursor position,
plus any of its subordinate levels.

1. Place insertion point anywhere in outline family.

2. Select Tools menu . . . . `Alt`+`T`

3. Select Outline . . . . `O`

4. Select Move Family . . . . `M`

   OR   **OR**

   Select Copy Family . . . . `C`

5. Press **arrow** keys until highlighted family
   is in desired outline position . . . . `⇅`

6. **Enter** . . . . `↵`

Delete Outline Family

1. Place insertion point anywhere in outline family.

2. Select Tools menu . . . . `Alt`+`T`

3. Select Outline . . . . `O`

4. Select Delete Family . . . . `E`

5. Select Yes . . . . `↵`

Change Outline Number Format

1. Place insertion point where new numbering format
   will begin.

2. Select Tools menu . . . . `Alt`+`T`

3. Select Outline . . . . `O`

4. Select Define . . . . `D`

5. Open Predefined Formats [⬦] . . . . `Alt`+`F`, `F4`
   and select desired format . . . . **letter**
   Paragraph, Outline, Legal (1.1.1), Bullets, User-Defined,

Continued ...

170

OUTLINE — Change Outline Number Format (continued)

If User-Defined was selected,

a) Select a level/style in **L**evel Style
list box . . . . `Alt`+`L`, `↑↓`

b) Select **S**tyle text box . . . . `Alt`+`S`

c) Type desired style character(s). . . . . . . **character(s)**

 OR   **OR**

 Open **S**tyle `◀` . . . . `F4`

 and select desired style . . . . **character**, `Space`

 1 Digits, A Uppercase Letters, a Lowercase Letters,
 I Uppercase Roman, i Lowercase Roman, X Uppercase Roman
 (digits if attached), x Lowercase Roman (digits if attached)

d) Repeat steps a-c for each level-style to define.

To attach or detach a level number style:
NOTE: *"1.a" is an example of an a level-two number (a)*
        attached to a level-one number (1).

a) Select a level/style to attach to previous
level in **L**evel Style list box . . . . `Alt`+`L`, `↑↓`

b) Select or clear ☐Attach **P**revious Level . . . `Alt`+`P`

 An * (asterisk) appears next level numbers that are attached.

6. Select **OK** . . . . `↵`

Change Starting Outline Number

1. Place insertion point where number will change.

2. Select **T**ools menu . . . . `Alt`+`T`

3. Select **O**utline . . . . `O`

4. Select **D**efine . . . . `D`

5. Select **St**arting Outline Number text box . . . . . `Alt`+`T`

6. Type starting number . . . . **number**

7. Select **OK** . . . . `↵`

171

Create a Style for Outline

1. Select **T**ools menu .... `Alt`+`T`
2. Select **O**utline .... `O`
3. Select **D**efine .... `D`
4. Select **C**hange .... `Alt`+`C`
5. Select **C**reate .... `Alt`+`C`
6. Type name of new style in **N**ame text box ..... **name**
7. Select **D**escription text box .... `Tab`
8. Type style description .... **description**
9. Select desired outline level
   in Define Outline Style list box ...... `Alt`+`L`, `↕`
10. Open **S**tyle Type [___ ◆] .... `Alt`+`S`, `F4`
    and select desired style type:
    - **O**pen .... `O`
    - **P**aired .... `P`

    If Paired was selected,
    a) Open Enter **K**ey [___ ◆] ...... `Alt`+`F`, `F4`
       and select desired enter key function .... **letter**
       Hard Return, Style Off, Style Off/On
       NOTE: *See Create a Style on page 235 for information about style types and Enter key options.*
11. Select **E**dit .... `Alt`+`E`
12. Insert format codes and text for outline level as desired.
13. Select **C**lose .... `Alt`+`C`
14. Repeat steps 9-13 for each outline level in the style.
15. Select **OK** .... `↵`
16. Select **C**lose .... `Alt`+`F4`
17. Select **OK** .... `Tab`, `↵`
    Press Tab until OK is outlined.

OUTLINE (continued)

Select Outline Style

1. Place insertion point where outline style will begin.
2. Select Tools menu .... `Alt`+`T`
3. Select Outline .... `O`
4. Select Define .... `D`
5. Select Change .... `Alt`+`C`
6. Select desired outline style in Name list box ... `N`, `↕`
7. Select Select .... `Alt`+`L`
8. Select OK .... `Tab`, `↵`
   Press Tab until OK is outlined.

OVERSTRIKE CHARACTERS

Create Overstrike Characters

Creates new characters by combining existing keyboard characters.

1. Place insertion point where overstrike character will be inserted.
2. Select Font menu .... `Alt`+`O`
3. Select Overstrike .... `V`
4. Select Create .... `C`

   If an attribute is to be used with the overstrike character(s),

   • Open Overstrike Characters `◄` .... `F4`
     and select desired attribute .... **letter**
5. Type desired characters .... **characters**
   Example: To create Ø, type O/.
6. Select OK .... `↵`

OVERSTRIKE CHARACTERS (continued)

Edit Overstrike Characters

1. Place insertion point after overstrike character to edit.
2. Select F**o**nt menu . . . . **Alt** + **O**
3. Select O**v**erstrike . . . . **V**
4. Select **E**dit . . . . **E**
5. Edit characters as desired.
6 Select OK . . . . **⏎**

PAGE BREAK

WordPerfect inserts a soft page break and inserts an single horizontal line when a page is filled with text. You can force a page break anywhere in your document as described below.

Insert a Hard Page Break

Ends current page, forces the start of a new page.

1. Place insertion point where new page will begin.
2. Press **Ctrl + Enter** (Page Break) . . . . **Ctrl** + **⏎**

   OR   **OR**

   Select **L**ayout menu . . . . **Alt** + **L**

   a) Select **P**age . . . . **P**

   b) Select **P**age Break . . . . **P**

A double horizontal line appears.

Delete Page Break

1. Place insertion point immediately below page break.
2. Press **Backspace** . . . . **BkSp**

OR

• Delete [HPg] code (see DELETE CODES on page 23).

PAGE NUMBERING

Page Number Position, Style, Accompanying Text

Turns on or off page numbering from insertion point forward; specifies position and style of page numbers; provides for adding accompanying text to page numbers.

1. Place insertion point where page numbering will begin.

2. Select <u>L</u>ayout menu . . . . **Alt** + **L**

3. Select <u>P</u>age . . . . **P**

4. Select <u>N</u>umbering . . . . **N**

To turn page numbering on (and specify its position) or turn page numbering off:

- Open <u>P</u>osition [⬚ ⬍] . . . . **Alt** + **P**, **F4**

  <u>and</u> select desired page number option . . . . **letter**

  <u>N</u>o Page Numbering, Top <u>L</u>eft, Top <u>C</u>enter, Top <u>R</u>ight, <u>A</u>lternating Top, <u>B</u>ottom Left, B<u>o</u>ttom Center, Bottom Right, Alt<u>e</u>rnating Bottom

To change page numbering style:

- Open Numbering <u>T</u>ype [⬚ ⬍] . . . . . **Alt** + **T**, **F4**

  <u>and</u> select desired page number style . . . . . . **character**

  <u>1</u>, 2, 3, 4 (Arabic), <u>i</u>, ii, iii, iv (Lowercase Roman), I, II, III, <u>IV</u> (Uppercase Roman)

To add accompanying text to page numbers:

a) Select <u>A</u>ccompanying Text text box . . . . **Alt** + **A**

b) Place insertion point before or after [^B] (page number code) and type desired text . . . **↹**, **text**

5. Select **OK** . . . . **↵**

NOTE: *You must preview (page 188) or print (page 184) the document to see page numbers.*

PAGE NUMBERING (continued)

New Page Number

Changes page numbering from insertion point forward.

1. Place insertion point where new page number will begin.

2. Select Layout menu .... `Alt` + `L`

3. Select Page .... `P`

4. Select Numbering .... `N`

5. Select New Page Number text box .... `Alt` + `N`

6. Type new page number .... **number**

7. Select OK .... `↵`

Insert Page Number Code

Inserts current page number code (^B) in document text at insertion point.
Preview or print document to see actual page number.

1. Place insertion point where page number code will appear.

2. Press **Ctrl + Shift + P** .... `Ctrl` + `Shift` + `P`

   OR   **OR**

   Select Layout menu .... `Alt` + `L`

   a) Select Page .... `P`

   b) Select Numbering .... `N`

   c) Select Insert Page Number .... `Alt` + `I`

The ^B character indicates where page number will appear when the
document prints.

176

Force Current Page to be Odd or Even

1. Place insertion point on page to change.
2. Select **L**ayout menu .... `Alt`+`L`
3. Select **P**age .... `P`
4. Select **N**umbering .... `N`
5. Select ☐**O**dd .... `Alt`+`O`

   OR   **OR**

   Select ☐**E**ven .... `Alt`+`E`
6. Select OK .... `↵`

PAPER SIZE

A paper size is a definition which specifies the paper type, size, and/or orientation for the printer you are using. It also controls other paper settings such as the location of the paper in the printer and double-sided printing.

Select an Existing Paper Definition

1. Select printer for which paper definition has been created.
2. Place insertion point at top of page where definition will take affect.
3. Select **L**ayout menu .... `Alt`+`L`
4. Select **P**age .... `P`
5. Select Paper **S**ize .... `S`
6. Select desired paper definition in **P**aper Type list box .. `¼`
7. Select **S**elect to return to document .... `↵`

PAPER SIZE (continued)

Create a Paper Definition

1. Select printer (page 194) for paper definition.

    NOTE: Your options will depend upon your printer's capability and the type of driver (Windows or WordPerfect) you have selected.

2. Select Layout menu .... `Alt`+`L`

3. Select Page .... `P`

4. Select Paper Size .... `S`

5. Select Add .... `Alt`+`A`

    To change the paper type:

    - Open Paper Type `[    ⬍]` .... `Alt`+`T`, `F4`

        and select desired paper type .... **letter**

        Standard, Bond, Letterhead, Labels, Envelope, Transparency, Cardstock, Other

        If Other was selected,

        1) If necessary, select Other text box ..... `Alt`+`H`

        2) Type name for paper type .... **text**

    To change the paper size:

    - Open Paper Size `[    ⬍]` .... `Alt`+`S`, `F4`

        and select desired paper size .... `↑/↓`, `Space`

        If "Other" or "User Defined" was selected,

        1) Select text box .... `Tab`

        2) Type paper width .... **number**

        3) Select text box .... `Tab`

        4) Type paper length .... **number**

    To prompt to load paper (WP driver only):

    - Select ☐Prompt to Load Paper .... `Alt`+`R`

    To use double-sided printing:

    - Select ☐Double Sided Printing .... `Alt`+`D`

Continued ...

178

To change the <u>paper orientation</u>:

- Click on desired orientation button.

  OR

  Select ☐<u>W</u>ide Form .... `Alt`+`W`

  AND/OR   **AND/OR**

  Select ☐Rot<u>a</u>ted Font .... `Alt`+`A`

To change the <u>paper location</u> in printer:

- Open Lo<u>c</u>ation `[____ ▼]` .... `Alt`+`C`, `F4`

  and select desired paper location .... **letter**

  Continuous, Manual, Bin

  If <u>B</u>in was selected,

  1) Select Bin <u>N</u>umber text box .... `Alt`+`N`

  2) Type bin number .... **number**

To specify direction of <u>binding offset</u>:

- Open B<u>i</u>nding `[____ ▼]` .... `Alt`+`I`, `F4`

  <u>and</u> select desired direction .... `↑↓`, `Space`

To <u>adjust where text prints</u> on paper (WP driver only):

a) Open To<u>p</u> `[____ ▼]` .... `Alt`+`P`, `F4`

   <u>and</u> select desired adjustment .... `↑↓`, `Space`

b) Select text box .... `Tab`

c) Type adjustment distance (inches) .... **number**

AND/OR   **AND/OR**

a) Open Sid<u>e</u> `[____ ▼]` .... `Alt`+`E`, `F4`

   <u>and</u> select desired adjustment .... `↑↓`, `Space`

b) Select text box .... `Tab`

c) Type adjustment distance (inches) .... **number**

6. Select **OK** .... `↵`

7. Select **Close** to return to document .... `Alt`+`F4`

PAPER SIZE (continued)

Edit Paper Definition

1. Select printer for which paper definition has been created.

   If editing a paper definition that is active,

   a) If necessary, turn Reveal Codes on ...... `Alt`+`F3`

   b) Place highlight immediately to the right of the [Paper Sz/Typ:...] code in your document.

2. Select **L**ayout menu .... `Alt`+`L`

3. Select **P**age .... `P`

4. Select Paper **S**ize .... `S`

5. Select desired paper definition in **P**aper Type list box .. `↕`

6. Select **E**dit .... `Alt`+`E`

7. Select desired options.
   See Create a Paper Definition on page 177, below step 5.

8. Select **OK** .... `↵`

9. Select **S**elect .... `Alt`+`S`
   to insert edited paper definition into document.

   OR   **OR**

   Select **Close** to return to document .... `Alt`+`F4`

180

Delete or Copy a Paper Definition

1. Select printer for which paper definition has been created.
2. Select Layout menu . . . . **Alt** + **L**
3. Select Page . . . . **P**
4. Select Paper Size . . . . **S**
5. Select desired paper definition in Paper Type list box . . **¼**

   To delete selected paper type:

   a) Select Delete . . . . **Alt** + **D**

   b) Select Yes to confirm deletion . . . . **Y**

   To copy selected paper type:

   a) Select Copy . . . . **Alt** + **C**

   b) Select desired options.

   See Create a Paper Definition on page 177, below step 5.

   NOTE: *You must rename the paper definition if you did not change the paper size.*

   c) Select **OK** . . . . **↵**
6. Select **Close** to return to document . . . . **Alt** + **F4**

PARAGRAPH NUMBERING

Use paragraph numbers to create an outline or number individual paragraphs. Paragraph numbering can incorporate up to eight levels to organize text hierarchically.

Paragraph Numbering

Numbers a paragraph according to the current paragraph numbering format. See Change Outline Number Format on page 169.

1. Place insertion point where paragraph number will be inserted.

2. Select <u>T</u>ools menu . . . . `Alt` + `T`

3. Select <u>O</u>utline . . . . `O`

4. Select <u>P</u>aragraph Number . . . . `P`

5. Select ○<u>A</u>uto (WordPerfect determines level) . . . . . . `A`

   OR   **OR**

   Select ○<u>M</u>anual (sets fixed level) . . . . `M`

   a) Select text box . . . . `Tab`

   b) Type outline level . . . . **number**

       NOTE: The outline level number will determine the number style.

6. Select <u>I</u>nsert . . . . `↵`

7. Repeat steps for each paragraph to number.

Change Paragraph Number Level

Changes paragraph number levels when numbering is set to auto (see above).

1. Place insertion point to left of paragraph number to change.

2. Press **Tab** . . . . `Tab`
   to increase numbering to next level.

   OR   **OR**

   Press **Shift** + **Tab** . . . . `Shift` + `Tab`
   to decrease numbering to previous level.

PASSWORD

Secures document from being opened, printed, or viewed by anyone who does not have the password. CAUTION: If you forget the password, you will not be able to open the document.

Create/Change Password

1. Open document (page 167) to protect.
2. Select File menu . . . . **Alt** + **F**
3. Select Password . . . . **W**
4. Type password . . . . **text**
   *WordPerfect displays a * (asterisk) for each character typed.*
5. Select Set . . . . **↵**
6. Re-type password . . . . **text**
7. Select Set to return to document . . . . **↵**
8. Save document (page 212).

NOTE: All associated backup files, buffer files, etc. will become password protected. Password protected files will not be searched in Find Files or Word Search without password entry.

Delete Password

1. Open password protected document (page 167).
2. Select File menu . . . . **Alt** + **F**
3. Select Password . . . . **W**
4. Select Remove . . . . **Alt** + **R**
5. Save document (page 212).

PASTE

Paste Contents of Clipboard

1. Place insertion point where Clipboard contents will be inserted.
2. Select Edit menu . . . . **Alt** + **E**
3. Select Paste . . . . **P**

PASTE (continued)

Undo Paste

NOTE: *You must undo a paste immediately after using the Paste command.*

1. Select Edit menu . . . . `Alt`+`E`
2. Select Undo . . . . `U`

PREFERENCES

Customizes initial settings for many WordPerfect features.

1. Select File menu . . . . `Alt`+`F`
2. Select Preferences . . . . `E`
3. Select desired option:

   Location of Files, Backup, Environment, Display, Print, Keyboard, Initial Codes, Document Summary, Date Format, Merge, Table of Authorities, Equations, Graphics Import

4. Select desired options for selection made.

   For further information, see topic headings:
   - *Location of Files on page 148.*
   - *Set Document Backup Options on page 3.*
   - *Environment Settings on page 44.*
   - *Display Settings on page 29.*
   - *Print Settings on page 189.*
   - *Keyboard Layout on pages 136-139.*
   - *Initial Codes on page 133.*

184

PRINT

WordPerfect provides the following ways to print your documents:

- *Print Current Document (see below).*
- *Print Multiple Pages of Current Document on page 185.*
- *Print Current Document on Disk on page 186.*
- *Print WordPerfect Document Files from File Manager on page 77.*

Also see Print Document Options on page 187.

Print Current Document

Prints full document, current page of document, or selected text in current document window.

1. If desired, select text (page 218) to print.

2. Select File menu . . . . `Alt`+`F`

3. Select Print . . . . `P`

4. Select one option:

   - Full Document . . . . `Alt`+`F`

   - Current Page . . . . `Alt`+`C`

   - Selected Text . . . . `Alt`+`L`

   To set other document print options:
   See Print Document Options on page 187.

5. Select Print . . . . `P`

Cancel a Print Job

Cancels print job while it is being sent to WordPerfect Print Manager.
NOTE: *Refer to your Windows documentation for information about cancelling a print job from Windows Print Manager.*

FROM CURRENT PRINT JOB DIALOG BOX

- Select Cancel Print Job . . . . `⏎`

PRINT (continued)

Print Multiple Pages of Current Document

1. Select File menu .... `Alt`+`F`
2. Select Print .... `P`
3. Select ○Multiple Pages .... `Alt`+`M`

   To set other document print options:
   See Print Document Options on page 187.
4. Select Print .... `Alt`+`P`
5. Type pages to print in Range text box .... **range**

Examples:	*(all)*	*prints entire document*
	-3	*prints pages 1 through 3*
	2,5	*prints pages 2 and 5*
	4-9	*prints pages 4 through 9*
	6-	*prints pages 6 to last page*
	-3,8-10,13	*prints pages 1-3, 8-10, 13*

   To print only odd or even pages:
   - Open Odd/Even [◆] .... `Alt`+`O`, `F4`

     and select desired option .... **letter**

     None, Odd, Even, Logical Odd, Logical Even

     NOTE: *Use Odd or Even to print every other page of document, regardless of page number. Use Logical Odd or Logical Even to print only those pages with odd or even page numbers. Select None to ignore Odd/Even printing.*

   To print document summary:
   - Select ☐Document Summary .... `Alt`+`D`
6. Select Print .... `↵`

PRINT (continued)

Print Current Document on Disk

Prints entire document or specified pages of a document file on disk.

1. Select File menu .... Alt + F
2. Select Print .... P
3. Select ○Document on Disk .... Alt + D

   To set other document print options:
   See Print Document Options on page 187.

4. Select Print .... ⏎
5. Type a filename in Filename text box .... **filename**

   OR   **OR**

   Open Filename File ▣ F4
   and select filename to print (pages 25, 26).

   To specify pages to print:

   a) Select Range text box .... Alt + R
   b) Type pages to print .... **range**

Examples:	(all)	*prints entire document*
	-3	*prints pages 1 through 3*
	2,5	*prints pages 2 and 5*
	4-9	*prints pages 4 through 9*
	6-	*prints pages 6 to last page*
	-3,8-10,13	*prints pages 1-3, 8-10, 13*

   To print only odd or even pages:

   • Open Odd/Even [◆] .... Alt + O , F4
     and select desired option .... **letter**
     None, Odd, Even, Logical Odd, Logical Even
     NOTE: *Use Odd or Even to print every other page of document, regardless of page number. Use Logical Odd or Logical Even to print only those pages with odd or even page numbers. Select None to ignore Odd/Even printing.*

   To print document summary:

   • Select ☐Document Summary .... Alt + D
6. Select Print .... ⏎

PRINT (continued)

Print Document Options

FROM PRINT DIALOG BOX

See Print Current Document on page 184.
See Print Multiple Pages of Current Document on page 185.
See Print Current Document on Disk on page 186.

To select a different printer:

1. Select **S**elect . . . . **Alt**+**S**

2. Select Printer Driver type:

   ○ **W**ordPerfect . . . . **Alt**+**W**

   ○ Wi**n**dows . . . . **Alt**+**N**

3. Select desired printer in
   Available Printers list . . . . **Alt**+**V**, **↕**

4. Select **S**elect . . . . **⏎**

To specify number of copies:

1. Select **N**umber of Copies increment box . . . . . . **Alt**+**N**

2. Type number of copies . . . . **number**

To set binding offset:

1. Select **B**inding Offset increment box . . . . **Alt**+**B**

2. Type space (inches) to adjust text . . . . **number**

To set graphics print quality:

• Open **G**raphics Quality [　♦] . . . . . . **Alt**+**G**, **F4**

   and select desired print quality . . . . **letter**

   High, Medium, Draft, Do Not Print, Set in Driver
   NOTE: *Options will depend on your printer selection.*

To set text print quality:

• Open **T**ext Quality [　♦] . . . . **Alt**+**T**, **F4**

   and select desired print quality . . . . **letter**

   High, Medium, Draft, Do Not Print, Set in Driver
   NOTE: *Options will depend on your printer selection.*

To initialize printer (download soft fonts to WP printer):

• Select **I**nitialize Printer . . . . **Alt**+**I**

188

PRINT PREVIEW

Displays document with headers, footers, fonts, page numbers, and other formatting that is not shown in document window.

1. Select File menu . . . . `Alt`+`F`
2. Select Print Preview . . . . `V`
3. Click on desired zoom or page button on button bar.

   OR

   To change view size of document:

   a) Select View menu . . . . `Alt`+`V`

   b) Select desired display option . . . . **character**
   *100%, 200%, Zoom In, Zoom Out, Zoom Area,
   Zoom to Full Width, Reset*

   To change page view of document:

   a) Select Pages menu . . . . `Alt`+`P`

   b) Select desired page view option . . . . **letter**
   Full Page, Facing Pages, Go to Page, Previous Page, Next Page

   If Go To Page was selected,

   a) Type page number . . . . **number**

   b) Select **OK** . . . . `↵`

4. Select **Close** . . . . `Alt`+`F`, `C`

PRINT SETTINGS (Preferences)

Sets default print settings.

NOTE: *You can override these setting for the current print job from the Print dialog box (page 187).*

1. Select File menu .... `Alt` + `F`
2. Select Preferences .... `E`
3. Select Print .... `P`

   To change multiple copies setting:

   a) Select Number of Copies increment box .... `Alt` + `N`

   b) Type number of copies .... **number**

   To specify generator of copies:

   • Open Generated By [▾] .... `Alt` + `B`, `F4`

     and select desired option .... **letter**

     WordPerfect, Printer

   To set binding offset:

   a) Select Binding Offset increment box .... `Alt` + `O`

   b) Type space (inches) to adjust text .... **number**

   To set graphics print quality:

   • Open Graphics Quality [▾] ..... `Alt` + `G`, `F4`

     and select desired print quality .... **letter**

     High, Medium, Draft, Do Not Print, Set in Driver

     NOTE: *Options will depend on your printer selection.*

   To set text print quality:

   • Open Text Quality [▾] .... `Alt` + `T`, `F4`

     and select desired print quality .... **letter**

     High, Medium, Draft, Do Not Print, Set in Driver

     NOTE: *Options will depend on your printer selection.*

Continued ...

PRINT SETTINGS — Preferences (continued)

To set redline option:

- Select one option:

    ○ **P**rinter Dependent .... `Alt`+`P`

    ○ Mar**k** Left Margin .... `Alt`+`K`

       1) Select **R**edline Character text box ... `Alt`+`R`

       2) Type redline character .... **text**

    ○ Mark **A**lternating Margins .... `Alt`+`A`

       1) Select **R**edline Character text box ... `Alt`+`R`

       2) Type redline character .... **text**

To set ratios of font size attributes to current font:

a) Select desired Size Attribute Ratio
increment box .... `Alt`+**letter**
Fine, Small, Large, Very Large, Extra Large, Super/Subscript

b) Type percentage of base font .... **number**

To set printing of graphics in fast mode:

- Select ☐Fa**s**t Graphics Printing .... `Alt`+`S`

4. Select **OK** to return to document .... `↵`

PRINTERS

Add a WordPerfect Printer

NOTE: *Before you can add a printer, you must first install the printer*
driver on your hard disk.

- *To add a <u>WordPerfect printer driver</u>, run WordPerfect's*
  Install program, select Custom, then select Printers.
- *To add a <u>Windows printer driver</u>, select the Printer icon from*
  the Windows Control Panel, then select Add. Refer to your
  Windows documentation for details.

1. Select File menu .... `Alt`+`F`

2. Select Select Printer .... `L`

3. Select ○ WordPerfect .... `Alt`+`W`

4. Select Add .... `Alt`+`A`

   To install a printer driver from existing All file:

   - Select ○ Additional Printers (*.all) .... `Alt`+`D`

   To select a previously installed printer:

   - Select ○ Printer Files (*.prs) .... `Alt`+`P`

5. Select desired printer in
   Available Printers list box .... `Alt`+`V`, `↹`

6. Select Add .... `↵`

   If installed from an All file,

   a) If desired, type new name for Prs file .... **text**

   b) Select **OK** .... `↵`

   NOTE: *To set up the printer, see Setup a Printer on page 195.*

7. Select **Close** to return to document .... `Alt`+`F4`

PRINTERS (continued)

Select Soft Fonts for a WordPerfect Printer

NOTE: This feature will only work if soft fonts have been installed.

1. Select File menu .... `Alt`+`F`

2. Select Select Printer .... `L`

3. Select ○ WordPerfect as printer driver ...... `Alt`+`W`

4. Select desired printer in
   Available Printers list box .... `Alt`+`V`, `↑↓`

5. Select Setup .... `Alt`+`E`

6. Select Cartridges/Fonts .... `Alt`+`C`

7. Select **Soft Fonts** in list box .... `↑↓`

8. Select Select .... `↵`

   If Font Groups dialog box appears,

   a) Select desired font family in Font Groups list ... `↑↓`

   b) Select Select .... `↵`

FROM SELECT FONTS DIALOG BOX

9. If necessary, select font list .... `Tab`
   Press Tab until list is selected.

10. Select font to mark in list box .... `↑↓`

11. Select □ * Present When Print Job Begins . `Shift`+`*`

    OR   **OR**

    Select □ ± Can be Loaded
    /Unloaded During Job .... `Shift`+`+`

12. Repeat steps 9-11 for each font to mark.

13. Select **OK** .... `↵`

    If Font Groups dialog box appears,

    • Repeat steps a and b, then steps 9-13.

      OR

      Select **Close** .... `Alt`+`F4`

Continued ...

PRINTERS — Select Soft Fonts for a WordPerfect Printer (continued)

14. Select **Close** .... `Alt`+`F4`
to close Cartridges and Fonts dialog box.

15. Select **OK** .... `Tab`, `↵`
Press Tab until OK is outlined.

16. Select **S**elect .... `↵`

Select Cartridge/Print Wheel for a WordPerfect Printer

NOTE: *This feature will only work if a cartridge or print wheel has been installed.*

1. Select **F**ile menu .... `Alt`+`F`

2. Select Se**l**ect Printer .... `L`

3. Select ○ **W**ordPerfect .... `Alt`+`W`

4. Select desired printer in
A**v**ailable Printers list box .... `Alt`+`V`, `↑↓`

5. Select S**e**tup .... `Alt`+`E`

6. Select **C**artridges/Fonts .... `Alt`+`C`

7. Select Cartridges or Print Wheel in list box ...... `↑↓`

8. Select **S**elect .... `↵`

FROM SELECT FONTS DIALOG BOX

9. Select desired cartridge or print wheel in list box ... `↑↓`

10. Select □* Present When Print Job Begins . `Shift`+`*`

11. Select **OK** .... `↵`

12. Select **Close** .... `Alt`+`F4`
to close Cartridges and Fonts dialog box.

13. Select **OK** .... `Tab`, `↵`
Press Tab until OK is outlined.

14. Select **S**elect .... `↵`

194

Select Printer

NOTE: *You must select a printer before printing a document.*

1. Select File menu .... **Alt** + **F**
2. Select Select Printer .... **L**
3. Select ○ WordPerfect printer driver .... **Alt** + **W**
   OR   **OR**
   Select ○ Windows printer driver .... **Alt** + **N**
4. Select a printer in
   Available Printers list box .... **Alt** + **V**, **↑↓**
   NOTE: *If desired printer is not in list,*
   see Add a WordPerfect Printer on page 191.
5. Select Select .... **↵**

Insert Printer Commands

Inserts a printer command in document.

1. Select a WordPerfect printer driver (page 194).
   NOTE: *Only WordPerfect printer drivers support this feature.*
2. Place insertion point where command will be inserted.
3. Select Layout menu .... **Alt** + **L**
4. Select Typesetting .... **N**
5. Select Printer Command .... **P**
6. Type printer command in
   Command text box .... **Tab**, command
   Refer to your printer's documentation.
7. Select OK .... **Tab**, **↵**
   Press Tab until OK is outlined.
8. Select OK to return to document .... **↵**

NOTE: *You cannot edit a printer command code. Instead, delete the*
code (page 23) and insert a new one.

PRINTERS (continued)

Set Up a Printer

Changes printer definition settings, including initial font, sheet feeder and port.

1. Select File menu .... `Alt`+`F`

2. Select Select Printer .... `L`

3. Select ◯ WordPerfect printer driver .... `Alt`+`W`

    OR   **OR**

    Select ◯ Windows printer driver .... `Alt`+`N`

4. Select desired printer
   in Available Printers list box .... `Alt`+`V`, `↑↓`

5. Select Setup .... `Alt`+`E`

    If WordPerfect printer driver was selected,

    To change displayed name of printer:

    • Type new name in Name text box .... **text**

    To change path for downloadable fonts:

    a) Select Path for Downloadable Fonts text box . `Alt`+`D`

    b) Type path to soft fonts .... **path**

       OR   **OR**

       Open Path for Downloadable Fonts ⊟ .... `F4`
       and select directory (pages 25, 26).

    To set initial font for printer:

    a) Select Initial Font .... `Alt`+`F`

    b) Select desired font .... `↑↓`

    c) Select OK .... `↵`

    To select a sheet feeder:

    a) Select Sheet Feeder .... `Alt`+`S`

    b) Select desired sheet feeder .... `↑↓`

    c) Select Select .... `↵`

Continued ...

196

To change printer port or destination of print job:

- Open **P**ort `[        ▼]` . . . . `Alt`+`P`, `F4`

  <u>and</u> select desired port . . . . **character**

  LPT 1, LPT 2, LPT 3, COM 1, COM 2, COM 3, COM 4, File

  ### If **F**ile (Print to Disk) was selected,

  - Type filename in **F**ilename text box . . . . . **filename**

  ### If printer is a network printer,

  - Select ☐**N**etwork Printer . . . . `Alt`+`E`

  NOTE: *Also see Select Soft Fonts for a WordPerfect Printer on*
  page 192 and Select Cartridge/Print Wheel for a WordPerfect
  Printer on page 193.

  ### If Windows printer driver was selected,
  The printer setup is controlled by Windows. Refer to your
  Windows documentation.

6. Select **OK** . . . . `↵`
7. Select **Close** to return to document . . . . `Alt`+`F4`

QUICK LIST

Add, Edit, Delete a Quick List Item
A Quick List item is a commonly used directory location which may
be given a descriptive name.

1. Select **F**ile menu . . . . `Alt`+`F`
2. Select **O**pen . . . . `O`
3. If necessary, select ☐**Q**uick List . . . . `Alt`+`Q`
4. Select **E**dit Quick List . . . . `Alt`+`E`

   ### To delete a Quick List item:

   a) Select item to delete in Quick List box . . . . `↑↓`
   b) Select **D**elete . . . . `Alt`+`D`
   c) Select **Y**es . . . . `↵`

Continued ...

QUICK LIST — Add, Edit, Delete a Quick List Item (continued)

To edit a Quick List item:

a) Select item to edit in Quick List box . . . . `↑⁄₄`

b) Select <u>E</u>dit . . . . `Alt` + `E`

To change directory location:

- Type directory name and or a filespec
  in Directory/Filename text box . . . . . **path\filespec**

  OR   **OR**

  Open <u>D</u>irectory/Filename ⊟ . . . . `F4`
  <u>and</u> select directory (pages 25, 26).

To change description:

1) Select Descriptive <u>N</u>ame text box . . . . `Tab`

2) Type new description for directory . . . . **text**

c) Select **OK** . . . . `↵`

To add an item to Quick List:

a) Select <u>A</u>dd . . . . `Alt` + `A`

b) Type directory name and or a filespec
   in Directory/Filename text box . . . . **path\filespec**

   OR   **OR**

   Open <u>D</u>irectory/Filename ⊟ . . . . `F4`
   <u>and</u> select directory (pages 25, 26).

c) Select Descriptive <u>N</u>ame text box . . . . `Tab`

d) Type description for directory . . . . **text**

e) Select **OK** . . . . `↵`

5. Select **OK** . . . . `↵`

6. Select **Cancel** to return to document . . . . `Tab`, `↵`
   *Press **Tab** until OK is outlined.*

QUICKFINDER *WP5.2*

Use the QuickFinder application to create indexes of your files and their contents. You can then specify a QuickFinder index to locate files with great speed.

Create QuickFinder Index

1. Run QuickFinder from Program Manager . . . . **QuickFinder File Indexer**
   Refer to your Windows documentation.

   If running QuickFinder for first time,

   - Select **OK** to accept proposed location of indexes . . ⏎

2. Select <u>C</u>reate . . . . **Alt**+**C**

3. Type a name to describe index . . . . **name**

4. Select **OK** . . . . ⏎

   To specify files to index <u>by typing</u>:

   a) Type directory and/or file pattern in
      Add <u>D</u>irectory or File text box . . . . **path\filespec**
      Example: c:\wp*.ltr *to specify only files with LTR filename extensions in the WP directory on drive C.*

   b) To include subdirectories of directory,

      - Select ☐<u>In</u>clude Subtree . . . . **Alt**+**N**

   c) Select <u>A</u>dd . . . . **Alt**+**A**

   d) Repeat steps a-c for each directory or
      file pattern to include in index.

   e) Select <u>I</u>ndex . . . . **Alt**+**I**

   f) Select **OK** . . . . ⏎

   g) Select other options or go to step 5 on page 200.

   Also see "To browse and select files to index" on the next page.

Continued ...

To browse and select files to index:

a) Select Bro<u>w</u>se . . . . `Alt`+`W`

To select a <u>drive</u>:

1) Open D<u>r</u>ives ◄ . . . . `Alt`+`R`, `F4`

   <u>an</u>d select desired drive letter . . . . `↕`, `F4`

   NOTE: *The "Add Directory or File" text box*
   shows current directory of selected drive.

2) Select directory for drive (see below).

   OR

   Select <u>A</u>dd . . . . `Alt`+`A`
   to add selection to Directories <u>t</u>o Index list.

To select a <u>directory</u> for current drive:

NOTE: *These steps require a mouse.*

1) Double-click on desired directory name in
   Di<u>r</u>ectories list box.

   NOTE: *To select a directory above the current directory,*
   double-click on [..] at top of list box.

2) Repeat step 1 until desired directory is selected.

   NOTE: *The Add Directory or File text box shows*
   selected directory.

3) To include files in all subdirectories of
   selected directory,

   • Select I<u>n</u>clude Subtree check box . . . `Alt`+`N`

4) Select <u>A</u>dd . . . . `Alt`+`A`
   to add selection to Directories <u>t</u>o Index list.

Continued ...

QUICKFINDER — Create QuickFinder Index (continued)

To select <u>specific files</u> in a directory:

1) Select drive and directory that contains files to index (previous page).

2) Select <u>F</u>ilename list box . . . . `Alt`+`F`

3) Select desired file to include in index . . . . `↑↓`

4) Select <u>A</u>dd . . . . `Alt`+`A`
   to add selection to Directories <u>t</u>o Index list.

5) Repeat steps 3 and 4 for each file to add.

To specify <u>specific files</u> in a directory <u>by typing</u>:

1) Select Add <u>D</u>irectory or File list box . . . . . `Alt`+`D`

2) Type directory and filespec . . . . **path\filespec**

3) To include files in all subdirectories of specified directory,

   • Select I<u>n</u>clude Subtree check box . . . `Alt`+`N`

4) Select <u>A</u>dd . . . . `Alt`+`A`

5) Repeat steps 2-4 for each filespec to add.

To select <u>Quick List directory items</u>:

1) Select <u>Q</u>uick List check box . . . . `Alt`+`Q`

2) Select Quick <u>L</u>ist list box . . . . `Alt`+`L`

3) Select desired item . . . . `↑↓`

4) Select <u>A</u>dd . . . . `Alt`+`A`
   to add selection to Directories <u>t</u>o Index list.

5) Repeat steps 3 and 4 for each item to add.

b) Select <u>I</u>ndex . . . . `Alt`+`I`

c) Select **OK** . . . . `↵`

5. Select **Close** to exit QuickFinder . . . . `Alt`+`F4`

Edit a QuickFinder Index

1. Run QuickFinder from Program Manager . . . . `WP` QuickFinder File Indexer
   Refer to your Windows documentation.

2. Select name of index to edit
   in Index **N**ames list box . . . . `Alt`+`N`, `↕`

3. Select **E**dit . . . . `Alt`+`E`

   To remove a directory from index:

   a) Select name of directory to remove in
      Directories **t**o Index list box . . . . `Alt`+`T`, `↕`

   b) Select Re**m**ove . . . . `Alt`+`M`

   To add a directory to index:
   See Create QuickFinder Index on page 198, below step 4.

4. Select **I**ndex . . . . `Alt`+`I`

5. Select ○**U**pdate Index With New or Modified File . . . . `U`

   OR   **OR**

   Select ○**I**ndex All Files . . . . `I`

6. Select **OK** to start indexing . . . . `↵`

7. Select **OK** . . . . `↵`

8. Select **Close** to exit QuickFinder . . . . `Alt`+`F4`

QUICKFINDER (continued)

Update a QuickFinder Index

1. Run QuickFinder from Program Manager . . . . QuickFinder File Indexer
   Refer to your Windows documentation.
2. Select name of index to update
   in Index **N**ames list box . . . . **Alt** + **N**, **↕**
3. Select **I**ndex . . . . **Alt** + **I**
4. Select ○ **U**pdate Index With New or Modified File . . . . **U**

   OR   **OR**

   Select ○ **I**ndex All Files . . . . **I**
5. Select **OK** . . . . **↵**
6. Select **OK** . . . . **↵**
7. Select **Close** to exit QuickFinder . . . . **Alt** + **F4**

Find Files from QuickFinder

1. Run QuickFinder from Program Manager . . . . QuickFinder File Indexer
   Refer to your Windows documentation.
2. Select **F**ind Files . . . . **Alt** + **F**
3. Follow steps below step 2 in Find Files on page 78.
4. Select **Close** to exit QuickFinder . . . . **Alt** + **F4**

QUICKFINDER (continued)

QuickFinder Index Options

QuickFinder options include: Information, Delete, Rename, Move, and Preferences.

1. Run QuickFinder from Program Manager .... `QuickFinder File Indexer`
   Refer to your Windows documentation.
2. Select desired index name in
   Index **N**ames list box .... `Alt`+`N`, `↑↓`
3. Open `Options ▼` .... `Alt`+`O`, `F4`

   and select desired index option:

   - _Information .... `I`
     - Select **OK** .... `↵`
   - **D**elete .... `D`
     - Select **Y**es to confirm .... `↵`
   - **R**ename .... `R`
     - a) Type name for index .... **name**
     - b) Select **OK** .... `↵`
   - **M**ove .... `M`
     - a) Type directory
       and/or filename .... **path** and/or **filename**
     - b) Select **OK** .... `↵`
   - **P**references .... `P`
     - a) Select options as desired.
     - b) Select **OK** .... `↵`
4. Select **Close** to exit QuickFinder .... `Alt`+`F4`

REDISPLAY SCREEN

Rewrites the screen to resolve jumbled display.

Press **Ctrl + F3** (Redisplay) . . . . `Ctrl` + `F3`

REDLINE/STRIKEOUT

Alters font to indicate text that has been added or text that can be deleted.

Redline/Strikeout Font

Also see Font Appearance/Size on page 85 and DOCUMENT COMPARE on page 31.

1. Select text (page 218) to redline.
2. Select F**o**nt menu . . . . `Alt` + `O`
3. Select **R**edline . . . . `R`

   OR   **OR**

   Select Stri**k**eout . . . . `K`
4. Press **Right** arrow to deselect text . . . . `→`

Set Printed Appearance of Redline Markings

Changes Redline printed appearance for current document only.

1. Select **L**ayout menu . . . . `Alt` + `L`
2. Select **D**ocument . . . . `D`
3. Select **R**edline Method . . . . `R`
4. Select desired Redline Method:

   O **P**rinter Dependent . . . . `P`

   O Mar**k** Left Margin . . . . `K`

   O Mark **A**lternating Margins . . . . `A`

   To change the redline character:

   a) Select **R**edline Character text box . . . . `Alt` + `R`

   b) Type new redline character . . . . **character**
5. Select **OK** to return to document . . . . `↵`

NOTE: See PRINT SETTINGS on pages 189 and 190 to set the default print appearance of Redline markings.

REPLACE

Finds and changes text and codes that match the search text.

Search and Replace Text or Codes

1. Place insertion point where search will begin.

   OR

   Select text (page 218) to search.

2. Select **E**dit menu . . . . **Alt**+**E**

3. Select **R**eplace . . . . **R**

4. Type text to search for in Search **F**or text box . . . . **text**

   AND/OR   **AND/OR**

   To insert a code to search for:

   a) Place insertion point in Search **F**or text box.

   b) Select **C**odes . . . . **Alt**+**C**

   c) Select desired code to search for . . . . **↕**

   d) Select **I**nsert . . . . **↵**

   e) Repeat steps a-d for each code to insert.

5. Select Replace **W**ith text box . . . . **Alt**+**W**

6. Type replacement text . . . . **text**

   AND/OR   **AND/OR**

   To insert a replacement code:

   a) Place insertion point in Replace **W**ith text box.

   b) Select **C**odes . . . . **Alt**+**C**

   c) Select desired replacement code . . . . **↕**

   d) Select **I**nsert . . . . **↵**

   e) Repeat steps a-d for each code to insert.

   To change direction of search:

   • Open **D**irection [＿＿＿ ↕] . . . . **Alt**+**D**, **F4**

     and select desired direction to search . . . . **letter**

     *F*orward, *B*ackward

Continued ...

REPLACE (continued)

To search only body of document:

- Select ☐Search Document **B**ody Only . . . . . `Alt`+`B`

To selectively search and replace:

a) Select Search **N**ext . . . . `Alt`+`N`
   Insertion point will stop at first search item.

b) Select **R**eplace . . . . `Alt`+`R`

   OR   **OR**

   Select Search **N**ext to retain item
   and continue search . . . . `Alt`+`N`

c) Repeat step b for each item found.

To globally replace all without prompting:

- Select Replace **A**ll . . . . `Alt`+`A`

7. Select **Close** to return to document . . . . `Alt`+`F4`

RETRIEVE DOCUMENT

Retrieves a file into the active document at insertion point location.

1. Place insertion point in document where file will be inserted.

2. Select **F**ile menu . . . . `Alt`+`F`

3. Select **R**etrieve . . . . `R`

4. Type filename in **F**ilename text box . . . . **filename**

   OR   **OR**

   Select filename in **F**iles list box . . . . `Alt`+`I`, `↕`
   See DIRECTORIES — LOCATING FILES on page 25.

5. Select **R**etrieve . . . . `↵`

6. Select **Y**es to insert file into current document . . . . . . `↵`

REVEAL CODES

Reveal Codes On/Off

Displays or hides document codes in a window at bottom of document.

- Press Alt + F3 (Reveal Codes) . . . . `Alt` + `F3`

   OR

   Drag ▬ (below vertical scroll bar) up to reveal codes.

   OR

   Drag reveal codes bar (double line) down below document window to hide codes.

   NOTE: Codes appear in a different color than ordinary text.

   To highlight a document code:

   - Click on code.

   OR

   - Press **arrow** keys until code is highlighted . . . . . . `↕`

Reveal Codes Colors

Changes colors of codes displayed in Reveal Codes.

1. Select File menu . . . . `Alt` + `F`
2. Select Preferences . . . . `E`
3. Select Display . . . . `D`
4. Select Reveal Codes Colors . . . . `Alt` + `R`
5. Select reveal codes item to change . . . . **letter**

   Text, Codes, Cursor

6. Select desired color for selected item
   in Foreground Palette . . . . `G`, `↹`, `Space`

   AND/OR   **AND/OR**

   Select desired color for selected item
   in Background Palette . . . . `A`, `↹`, `Space`

7. Repeat steps 5 and 6 for each item to change.
8. Select **OK** . . . . `↵`
9. Select **OK** to return to document . . . . `Tab`, `↵`

   Press Tab until OK is outlined.

RULER

Use the ruler to easily format your document with a mouse.

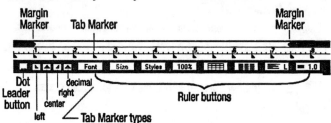

Margin Marker   Tab Marker   Margin Marker

Dot Leader button | center | left — Tab Marker types | decimal right   Ruler buttons

Ruler On/Off

Displays or hides ruler at top of document. Also see ENVIRONMENT SETTINGS, pages 44 and 45 to set ruler to appear each time you start.

1. Select <u>V</u>iew menu .... **Alt**+**V**

2. Select or deselect <u>R</u>uler .... **R**

Set Left and Right Margins using the Ruler

1. Place insertion point on line where new margin will begin.

2. Drag margin marker .... ▶ or ◀
   to desired position on ruler.

Change Tab Setting using the Ruler

• Place insertion point where tab adjustment will begin.

   To adjust a tab stop:

   • Drag tab marker to desired position on ruler.

   To add a tab stop of a specific type:

   If adding a dot leader tab,

   • Click on Dot Leader button.

   • Drag a tab marker type to desired position on ruler.

   To delete a tab stop:

   • Drag tab marker below ruler.

RULER (continued)

Add Fonts to Font Button on Ruler

Adds fonts to Font pop-up list available from ruler.

1. Double-click on . . . . `Font`

2. Click on . . . . **Assign to Ruler...**

3. Double-click on desired font in Font List box.
   WordPerfect adds font to Fonts on Ruler list.

4. Repeat step 3 for each font to add.

5. Click on . . . . `OK`

6. Click on . . . . `OK`

Select Font using the Ruler

1. Place insertion point where font change will begin.

   OR

   Select text (page 218) to change.

2. Click . . . . `Font`
   <u>and</u> drag highlight to desired font.

Change Font Size using the Ruler

Changes size of scalable fonts only.

1. Place insertion point where new point size will begin.

   OR

   Select text (page 218) to change.

2. Click . . . . `Size`
   <u>and</u> drag highlight to desired point size.

Justify Text using the Ruler

1. Place insertion point where new justification will begin.
   OR
   Select text (page 218) to justify.

2. Click . . . . `≡ L`
   <u>and</u> drag highlight to desired justification type.
   Left, Right, Center, Full

RULER (continued)

Apply a Style using the Ruler

1. Place insertion point where style will begin.

   OR

   Select text (page 218) to format.

2. Click . . . . `Styles`
   and drag highlight to desired style.

Create Columns using the Ruler

Creates from two to five evenly-spaced newspaper columns.

1. Place insertion point where columns will begin.

   OR

   Select text (page 218) to include in columns.

2. Click . . . . �(columns icon)
   and drag highlight to desired number of columns.

Adjust Column Widths using the Ruler

1. Place insertion point anywhere in a column.

2. Drag desired column margin marker . . . . ► or ◄
   to desired position on ruler.

Turn Columns Off using the Ruler

1. Place insertion point where columns will end.

2. Click . . . . ▐(columns icon)
   and drag highlight to . . . . **Columns Off**

Create Tables using the Ruler

1. Place insertion point where table will begin.

2. Click . . . . ▐(table icon)
   and drag highlight over cells until desired size is obtained.

RULER (continued)

Adjust Table Margins using the Ruler

1. Place insertion point anywhere within table.

2. Drag table's margin marker . . . . ▶ or ◀
   to desired position on ruler.

Adjust Table Column Widths using the Ruler

To adjust column width and all columns to right without changing table size:

- Drag desired table's column marker . . . . ▼
  to desired position on ruler.

To adjust column width and next column without changing table size:

- Press and hold **Shift** . . . . `Shift`
  <u>and</u> drag column marker . . . . ▼

To adjust column width and move all columns to the right:

- Press and hold **Ctrl** . . . . `Ctrl`
  <u>and</u> drag column marker . . . . ▼

Change Line Spacing using the Ruler

1. Place insertion point where new line height will begin.
   OR
   Select text (page 218) to change.

2. Click . . . . `≡ 1.0`
   <u>and</u> drag highlight to desired option.
   1.0, 1.5, 2.0

Change Zoom Level using the Ruler

- Click . . . . `100%`
  <u>and</u> drag highlight to desired zoom setting.
  50%, 75%, 100%, 150%, 200%, Page Width

212

SAVE

Save New Document and Continue Working

1. Select File menu . . . . `Alt`+`F`

2. Select Save . . . . `S`

3. Type a filename in Save As text box . . . . **filename**
   > **NOTE:** If necessary, type path to file.
   > **Example:** *c:\wpwin\docs\filename.*

4. Select Save . . . . `⏎`

Save New Document and Exit WordPerfect

1. Select File menu . . . . `Alt`+`F`

2. Select Exit . . . . `X`

3. Select Yes . . . . `Y`

4. Type a filename in Save As text box . . . . **filename**
   > **NOTE:** If necessary, type path to file.
   > **Example:** *c:\wpwin\docs\filename.*

5. Select Save . . . . `⏎`

Save Document Again and Continue Working

1. Select File menu . . . . `Alt`+`F`

2. Select Save . . . . `S`

Save Document Again and Exit WordPerfect

1. Select File menu . . . . `Alt`+`F`

2. Select Exit . . . . `X`

3. Select Yes to save changes to file . . . . `Y`

Save Selected Text as New Document

1. Select text (page 218) to save.

2. Select File menu . . . . `Alt`+`F`

3. Select Save As . . . . `A`

4. Type a filename in Save As text box . . . . **filename**
   > **NOTE:** If necessary, type path to file.
   > **Example:** *c:\wpwin\docs\filename*

5. Select Save . . . . `⏎`

SEARCH

1. Place insertion point where search will begin.
   OR
   Select text (page 218) to search.
2. Select **E**dit menu . . . . **Alt** + **E**
3. Select **S**earch . . . . **S**
4. Type text to search for in Search **F**or text box . . . . . **text**

   To insert a code to search for:
   NOTE: *The Any Char code can be used as a wildcard. You can use it as a substitute for any character, tab, or space.*

   a) Place insertion point in Search **F**or text box.
   b) Select **C**odes . . . . **Alt** + **C**
   c) Select desired code to search for . . . . **↑/↓**
   d) Select **I**nsert . . . . **↵**
   e) Repeat steps a-d for each code to insert.

   To change direction of search:
   • Open **D**irection [⬍] . . . . **Alt** + **D**, **F4**
   and select desired direction to search . . . . **letter**
   *F*orward, *B*ackward

   To search only body of document:
   • Select ☐Search Document **B**ody Only . . . . **Alt** + **B**
5. Select **S**earch . . . . **Alt** + **S**

Insertion point moves to first occurrence of item in direction specified.

Search for Next/Previous Occurrence of Last Search

1. Select **E**dit menu . . . . **Alt** + **E**
2. Select Search Ne**x**t . . . . **X**
   OR   **OR**
   Select Searc**h** Previous (*WP5.2*) . . . . **H**
   OR   **OR**
   Select Search Pre**v**ious (*WP5.1*) . . . . **V**

SELECT DIALOG BOX ITEMS

Select Text Box

A text box is a rectangular box in which you can type information such as a filename. When selected, the existing text is highlighted or a flashing cursor appears.

- Click in text box . . . . ⬚

OR

- Press **Tab** until text box is selected . . . . **Tab**

OR   **OR**

- Press **Alt** + underlined letter
  in text box name . . . . **Alt** + letter

Select Increment Box and Enter a Value

An increment box is a text box in which you can type values or select values by clicking on its increment arrows. When selected, the existing value is highlighted or a flashing cursor appears.

1. Click in increment box . . . . ⬚⬍

2. Type value.

OR

- Click on **up** or **down** increment arrow . . . . ⬍
  until desired value appears.

OR

1. Press **Tab** until increment box is selected . . . . **Tab**

   OR   **OR**

   Press **Alt** + underlined letter
   in increment box name . . . . **Alt** + letter

2. Type value.

SELECT — Select Dialog Box Items (continued)

Open a List Button ⊟

A list button is an icon that appears to the right of certain text boxes. These buttons can be opened to access another dialog box from which a drive, directory, or filename can be selected.

1. Click on .... ⊟

2. Make selections in dialog box as desired.

OR

1. Press **Tab** until text box with list button is selected .. `Tab`

   OR   **OR**

   Press **Alt + underlined letter**
   in name of text box .... `Alt` + **letter**

2. Press **F4** .... `F4`

3. Make selections in dialog box as desired.

Open a Pop-Up Button [◆] and Select Item

Opens a pop-up list from which selections can be made. Most pop-up buttons display the current selection and are marked with up and down arrows. Some pop-up buttons are named and are marked by a single arrow (Options ▼).

• Click .... [◆]
  and drag highlight to desired item.

OR

1. Press **Alt + underlined letter**
   in pop-up button name .... `Alt` + **letter**

2. Press **F4** to open list box .... `F4`

3. Press underlined letter in option name .... **letter**

   OR   **OR**

   a) Press **Up** or **Down** arrow to highlight item ..... `↕`

   b) Press **Space** to select item .... `Space`

SELECT — Select Dialog Box Items (continued)

Select Item in a List Box
A list box contains all available choices for a specific list.
• Click on item in list box.

OR

1. Press **Alt + underlined letter**
   in list box name . . . . **Alt** + letter
2. Press **Up** or **Down** arrow until item is highlighted . . . **↑↓**

Open a Drop-Down List ⬇ and Select Item
Opens a drop-down list from which selections can be made.
Current selection appears to left of drop-down arrow.

1. Click on . . . . **⬇**
2. Click on item.

OR

1. Press **Alt + underlined letter**
   in list box name . . . . **Alt** + letter
2. Press **F4** to open list box **F4**
3. Press **Up** or **Down** arrow to highlight item . . . . **↑↓**
4. Press **F4** to select item **F4**

Select a Command Button
A command button executes a specific command.
• Click on command button.

OR

• Press **Alt + underlined letter**
  in command name . . . . **Alt** + letter

OR   **OR**

1. Press **Tab** . . . . **Tab**
   until command button is outlined.
2. Press **Enter** . . . . **↵**

SELECT — Select Dialog Box Items (continued)

Select or Clear Check Box ☒

Check boxes options can be switched on or off. More than one check box may be selected within a group. A selected check box contain an X.

* Click on .... ☒
  to clear and turn option off.

  OR   **OR**

  Click on .... ☐
  to select and turn option on.

OR

* Press **Alt + underlined letter**
  in check box name to select or clear ...... **Alt** + **letter**

Select Radio Button ⦿

Only one radio button may be selected within a group. A selected radio button contains a dark circle.

* Click on .... ○

OR

* Press **Alt + underlined letter**
  in option name .... **Alt** + **letter**

SELECT MENU ITEM

Select Menu Item with Mouse

1. Click on menu name that contains item.

2. Click on menu item.

Select Menu Item With Keyboard

1. Press **Alt + underlined letter**
   in menu name that contains item .... **Alt** + **letter**

2. Press **underlined letter** of menu item .... **letter**

SELECT TEXT

Select Text with Mouse
Select text block
• Drag highlight through text.

Select word
• Double-click on word.

Select sentence
• Triple-click on any word in sentence.

Select paragraph
• Quadruple-click on any word in paragraph.

Select from insertion point to specified location
1. Click on starting position in text.
2. Press **Shift** .... `Shift`
   <u>and</u> click on ending position in text.

End Text Selection with Mouse
• Click anywhere in document.

Select Sentence or Paragraph using Menu
1. Place insertion point anywhere within sentence or paragraph to select.
2. Select <u>E</u>dit menu .... `Alt`+`E`
3. Select S<u>e</u>lect .... `E`
4. Select <u>S</u>entence .... `S`
   OR   **OR**
   Select <u>P</u>aragraph .... `P`

SELECT TEXT (continued)

Select Rectangular Sections of Text

Selects specific columns of text when columns are separated by spaces and each line ends with a hard return.

1. Select text area that marks upper left corner and lower right corner of rectangular section of text.
   Selection includes column you want and parts of all columns.

2. Select **E**dit menu .... `Alt`+`E`

3. Select S**e**lect .... `E`

4. Select **R**ectangle .... `R`

Selection shows only columns indicated by upper left and lower right corners of selection.

Select Tabular Columns

Select specific columns of text when columns are separated by tabs or indents and each line ends with a hard return.

1. If necessary, turn Reveal Codes on .... `Alt`+`F3`

2. Select text area that marks upper left corner and lower right corner of column to select.
   Selection includes column you want and parts of all columns.

3. Select **E**dit menu .... `Alt`+`E`

4. Select S**e**lect .... `E`

5. Select **T**abular Column .... `T`

Selection shows only columns indicated by upper left and lower right corners of selection.

Select Text Using Select Mode

1. Place insertion point where selection will begin.

2. Press **F8** (CUA) . . . . `F8`
   to begin Select Mode.

   OR   **OR**

   Press **F12** (WP 5.1 DOS) . . . . `F12`
   to begin Select Mode.

   To expand selection to any character in document:

   - Type a character . . . . **character**
     Example: To select to end of sentence, press . (period).

   **To expand selection using insertion point, page,
   or screen movement keys:**

   - Press key.
     Example: To extend selection one page up, press PgUp.

3. Press **F8** (CUA) . . . . `F8`
   to end Select Mode.

   OR   **OR**

   Press **F12** (WP 5.1 DOS) . . . . `F12`
   to end Select Mode.

SELECT TEXT (continued)

Other Text Selection Methods with CUA Keyboard

One character to the left or right . . . . **Shift** + ◄►

One line up or down . . . . **Shift** + ▲▼

End of line (after codes) . . . . **Shift** + **End**

Beginning of line (after codes) . . . . **Shift** + **Home**

Beginning of line
(before codes) . . . . **Shift** + **Home**, **Shift** + **Home**

To top of screen . . . . **Shift** + **PgUp**

To bottom of screen . . . . **Shift** + **PgDn**

To first line on previous page . . . . **Shift** + **Alt** + **PgUp**

To first line on next page . . . . **Shift** + **Alt** + **PgDn**

One word to the left or right . . . . **Shift** + **Ctrl** + ◄►

One paragraph up or down . . . . **Shift** + **Ctrl** + ▲▼

To beginning of document
(after codes) . . . . **Shift** + **Ctrl** + **Home**

To beginning of document
(before codes) . . **Shift** + **Ctrl** + **Home**, **Shift** + **Ctrl** + **Home**

To end of document
(after codes) . . . . **Shift** + **Ctrl** + **End**

SORT

Arranges text alphabetically or numerically by line, paragraph, secondary merge records, or sorts rows in a table.

Sort Contents of a Document

1. Place insertion point anywhere in document
   to sort <u>entire document</u>.

   OR

   Select lines of text or rows in table
   to sort <u>part of document or table</u>.

   OR

   Place insertion point anywhere within table
   to sort <u>all rows in a table</u>.

2. Select <u>T</u>ools menu . . . . **Alt** + **T**

3. Select So<u>r</u>t . . . . **R**

4. Select desired sort type . . . . **Alt** +letter
   Line, Paragraph, Merge Record, Table Row

5. Select desired sort order . . . . **Alt** +letter
   Ascending, Descending

   To <u>specify key definition</u> for sort:

   a) Open Key Type [___ ⬦] . . . . **Alt** +number, **F4**
      Where number is the number of key you are defining.
      <u>and</u> select option:

      - Select <u>A</u>lpha . . . . **A**
        OR   **OR**
        Select <u>N</u>umeric . . . . **N**

   b) Specify the key's position in record
      (field, line, word) . . . . **Tab**, number

   c) Repeat step b as needed.
      NOTE: See example and definitions on next page.

   To <u>add a new key</u>:

   - Select <u>A</u>dd Key . . . . **Alt** + **A**

Continued ...

SORT (continued)

To <u>insert a new key</u>:

a) Select a text box in key, below
   which new key will be inserted. . . **Alt** + number, **Tab**

b) Select Insert Key . . . . **Alt** + **I**

To <u>delete a key</u>:

a) Select any text box in
   key to delete . . . . **Alt** + number, **Tab**

b) Select **D**elete Key . . . . **Alt** + **D**

6. Select **OK** to sort . . . . **↵**

Example of key definitions and how it would sort line records:

Key Definitions

Key	Type	Field	Line	Word
<u>1</u>	Alpha	1	1	1
<u>2</u>	Alpha	1	1	2

*Sorts records alphabetically by the first word in field one.
Then in the event of a tie, WordPerfect would look at the
<u>second word</u> in first field to determine the sort order.*

Result:

Field 1	Field 2	Field 3	F4	Field 5
▼	▼	▼	▼	▼
Bruno, Carmine	25 Steig Ave	New York,	NY	212-966-7321
Pinto, Frank	455 Davis Ave	Staten Island,	NY	718-967-1234
Spohn, <u>Bill</u>	123 Main St	Princeton,	NJ	201-555-1515
Spohn, <u>Ziggi</u>	111 Paul Ave	Staten Island,	NY	718-351-5555
Stokes, Dom	392 Katan Ave	Hollywood,	CA	213-966-9788

*Each field in a line record is separated by a tab, and each record by
a return.*

NOTE: *A Key Definition tells WordPerfect how to sort.*

- *The **Key** type specifies if the data is numeric or alphabetic.*
- *The **Field** entry specifies which tab stop or field in a
  secondary record file to use as the sort key.*
- *The **Word** entry specifies which word in the field to use as
  the sort key.*
- *The **Line** entry specifies which line in a record to use as the
  sort key.*
- *The **Cells** entry specifies the cell in a table to use as the
  sort key.*

You can have as many as nine sort keys in a Key Definition.

224

SORT (continued)

Extract Records

Extracts records that meet a specified criteria from your document.

1. Before beginning, save document containing records
   to extract.

   NOTE: *After you extract records, the document will only contain the
   records you specify in this process.*

2. Place insertion point anywhere in document
   to select from <u>all records in document</u>.

   OR

   Select text (page 218) from which records will be extracted.

3. Select **T**ools menu .... **Alt** + **T**

4. Select So**r**t .... **R**

5. Select desired sort type .... **Alt** +**letter**

   Line, **P**aragraph, **M**erge Record, **T**able Row, **N**o Sort

   NOTE: *Select **N**o Sort if you do not want to sort extracted records.*

6. Specify key definition for sort (see page 222, below step 5).

7. Select **R**ecord Selection text box .... **Alt** + **R**

8. Type a selection statement for records to extract ..... **text**

   Example: *key1=Jones + key3=New York selects records*
   *that have Jones for key1 **or** New York for key3.*
   Also see Selection Statement — Operators and Examples on next page.

9. Select **OK** .... **↵**

Only records that met criteria remain in document or selection area.

SORT (continued)

Selection Statement — Operators and Examples

Use the following operators and examples as a guide for entering a selection statement (step 8 on previous page) that will extract the records you want.

Operators:	Description:
+	Selects records that meet conditions of either key.
	Example: key1=Jones + key3=New York selects records that have Jones for key1 **or** New York for key3.
*	Selects records that meet conditions of **both** records.
	Example: key1=Jones * key3=New York selects only those records that have Jones for key1 and New York for key3.
=	Selects records that exactly **match** condition of statement.
	Example: key1=Jones selects only those records that have Jones for key1.
<>	Selects records that **do not equal** condition of statement.
	Example: key1<>Jones selects every record except those that have Jones for key1.
>	Selects records that have a value **greater than** the condition of the statement.
	Example: key1>Jones selects records with a key1 value alphabetically greater than Jones.
<	Selects records that have a value **less than** the condition of the statement.
	Example: key1<Jones selects records with a key1 value alphabetically less than Jones.
>=	Selects records that have a value **greater than** or equal to the condition of the statement.
	Example: key1>=Jones selects records with a key1 value alphabetically equal to or greater than Jones.
<=	Selects records that have a value **less than or equal** to the condition of the statement.
	Example: key1<=Jones selects records with a key1 value alphabetically equal to or less than Jones.

SPECIAL CODES

Use this feature to insert special formatting codes, such as hard tabs, dot leaders, hyphens, and other codes into your document.

1. Place insertion point where code will be inserted.

2. Select **L**ayout menu .... `Alt`+`L`

3. Select **L**ine .... `L`

4. Select Special C**o**des .... `O`

5. Select desired Special Codes option:

Hard Tab Codes:

○ **L**eft [HdTab] .... `L`

○ **C**enter [HdCntrTab] .... `C`

○ **R**ight [HdRgtTab] .... `R`

○ **D**ecimal [HdDecTab] .... `D`

Hard Tab Codes with Dot Leaders

○ L**e**ft [HdTab] .... `E`

○ Ce**n**ter [HdCntrTab] .... `N`

○ Righ**t** [HdRgtTab] .... `T`

○ Deci**m**al [HdDecTab] .... `M`

Hyphenation Codes

○ **H**yphen [-] .... `H`

○ D**a**sh Character .... `A`

○ **S**oft Hyphen - .... `S`

○ Hyphenation So**f**t Return [HyphSRt] .... `F`

○ Hyphenation Ignore **W**ord [HyphIgnWrd] .... `W`

Continued ...

SPECIAL CODES (continued)

Other Codes

O Hard Space [HdSpc] .... **P**

O End Centering/Alignment [EndC/A] .... **/**

O Decimal Align Character .... **G**

To change decimal character:

a) Select text box .... **Tab**

b) Type desired character .... **character**

OR   **OR**

To change thousands separator character:

a) Select Thousands Separator text box .... **Tab**

b) Type desired character .... **character**

6. Select Insert .... **↵**

SPELLER

Checks document for misspelled words, words repeated twice in a row, and certain capitalization errors.

Spell-Check a Document

If checking part of document,

- Select text (page 218) to spell-check.

1. Select <u>T</u>ools menu . . . . `Alt`+`T`
2. Select <u>S</u>peller . . . . `S`

   To specify part of document to check:

   a) Select Chec<u>k</u> menu (*WP5.2*) . . . . `Alt`+`K`

   b) Select part of document to check . . . . **letter**
      <u>W</u>ord, <u>D</u>ocument, To <u>E</u>nd of Document, <u>P</u>age,
      To En<u>d</u> of Page, <u>S</u>elected Text, <u>T</u>ext Entry Box, To End of Te<u>x</u>t

   OR   **OR**

   - Open Chec<u>k</u> [____ ▼] (*WP5.1*) . . . . . `Alt`+`K`, `F4`

      <u>and</u> select part of document to check . . . . **letter**
      <u>W</u>ord, <u>D</u>ocument, To <u>E</u>nd of Document, <u>P</u>age,
      To En<u>d</u> of Page, <u>S</u>elected <u>T</u>ext, To End of <u>S</u>election

3. Select S<u>t</u>art . . . . `Alt`+`T`
4. When Speller stops and highlights a word,
   select one of the following:

   To add word to dictionary and continue checking:

   - Select <u>A</u>dd . . . . `Alt`+`A`

   To skip this occurrence of word only:

   - Select Skip <u>O</u>nce . . . . `Alt`+`O`

   To skip this word and any other occurrences:

   - Select Skip A<u>l</u>ways . . . . `Alt`+`L`

   To replace word with a suggested word:

   a) Select desired word in Suggestions list box . . . . . `⇅`

   b) Select <u>R</u>eplace . . . . `↵`

   To suggest a spelling for a word:
   See Suggest a Spelling on page 231, steps 3-5.   **Continued ...**

SPELLER — Spell-Check a Document (continued)

If consecutive duplicate words are found,

Select one of the following:

☐ **D**isable Checking .... D
   to ignore duplicate words.

• **C**ontinue C
   to continue spell-checking and leave
   both words in document.

• Delete **2**nd 2
   to delete second occurrence of word and
   continue spell-checking.

If irregular capitalization is found,

*Occurs when word falls into one of the following five
example patterns: THat, tHat, tHAT, thAt, aT (two-letter word)*

Select one of the following:

☐ **D**isable Checking .... D
   to ignore irregular capitalization.

• **C**ontinue C
   to continue spell-checking without changing word.

• **R**eplace .... R
   to replace irregular capitalization with proper
   capitalization.

5. Repeat step 4 for each misspelled word.

6. Select **Y**es (*WP5.2*) .... ⏎

   OR   **OR**

   Select OK (*WP5.1*) .... ⏎

   • Select **C**lose to return to document .... ⏎

SPELLER (continued)

Change Dictionary

1. Select **T**ools menu . . . . **Alt** + **T**
2. Select **S**peller . . . . **S**
3. Select **D**ictionary menu . . . . **Alt** + **D**
4. Select **M**ain . . . . **M**

   OR   **OR**

   Select **S**upplementary . . . . **S**
5. Type directory and filename of dictionary
   in **F**ilename text box . . . . **path\filename**

   OR   **OR**

   Select dictionary filename
   in F**i**les list box . . . . **Alt** + **I** , **↓**

   See DIRECTORIES — LOCATING FILES on page 25.

   NOTE: *The filename of the main dictionary is*
   "wp{wp}us.lex". Supplementary dictionaries have a
   file extension of ".sup". See LOCATION OF FILES on
   page 148 for default location of dictionary files.
6. Select **Select** . . . . **↵**
7. Select **C**lose to return to document . . . . **Alt** + **C**

SPELLER (continued)

Suggest a Spelling

1. Select **T**ools menu . . . . `Alt`+`T`
2. Select **S**peller . . . . `S`
3. Type a <u>word pattern</u> in Replace **W**ith text box (*WP5.2*) **text**

   OR   **OR**

   Select **W**ord text box (*WP5.1*) . . . . `Alt`+`W`

   - Type a <u>word pattern</u> . . . . **text**

   NOTE: *In a <u>word pattern</u>, a question mark (?) represents a single character and an asterisk (*) represents multiple characters. For example the? suggests **then** and **them**, while he* suggests **her**, **here**, and **hear**.*

4. Select **S**uggest . . . . `Alt`+`S`
5. View suggestions or select other options if performing a spell-check.
6. Select **C**lose to return to document . . . . `Alt`+`C`

Set Speller Options

1. Select **T**ools menu . . . . `Alt`+`T`
2. Select **S**peller . . . . `S`
3. Select O**p**tions menu . . . . `Alt`+`P`
4. Select or deselect speller option:

   - Words with **N**umbers . . . . `N`
     Deselect to ignore words that contain numbers.
   - **D**uplicate Words . . . . `D`
     Deselect to ignore consecutive duplicate words.
   - **I**rregular Capitalization . . . . `I`
     Deselect to ignore irregular capitalization.
   - **M**ove to Bottom (*WP5.1*) . . . . `M`
     Select to position Speller window at bottom of screen.
   - Display **S**uggestions (*WP5.2*) . . . . `S`

5. Repeats steps 3 and 4 to set additional options.
6. Select **C**lose to return to document . . . . `Alt`+`C`

SPREADSHEETS

You can import or establish links to the following spreadsheet formats:
PlanPerfect v3.0 - v5.1, Lotus 1-2-3 v1.0 - v3.1,
Microsoft Excel v2.0 - v3.0, Quattro and Quattro Pro.
NOTE: *The maximum number of spreadsheet columns is thirty-two.*

Import a Spreadsheet

Copies data from a spreadsheet into current document. Also see Create or Edit Link to a Spreadsheet on next page.

1. Place insertion point where spreadsheet file will be inserted.

2. Select **T**ools menu . . . . **Alt**+**T**

3. Select Spr**e**adsheet . . . . **E**

4. Select **I**mport . . . . **I**

5. Type filename of spreadsheet to import
   in **F**ilename text box . . . . **filename**
   NOTE: *If necessary, type path to file.*
         Example: *C:\123\123191.WKS*

   OR   **OR**

   Open **F**ilename **e** **F4**
   and select filename (pages 25, 26).

   To limit import to a range in spreadsheet:

   a) Select **R**ange text box . . . . **Alt**+**R**

   b) Type range of cells . . . . **range**
       Example: *A1:B20*
   OR   **OR**

   Select a range name in
   Range **N**ame list box . . . . **Alt**+**N**, **↑↓**

6. Select ○**T**able . . . . **Alt**+**T**
   to import spreadsheet as a WordPerfect table.

   OR   **OR**

   Select ○Te**x**t . . . . **Alt**+**X**
   to import spreadsheet as text.

7. Select **OK** . . . . **↵**

SPREADSHEETS (continued)

Create or Edit Link to a Spreadsheet

Copies spreadsheet data into current document and updates the data when changes are made to the source spreadsheet file.

1. Place insertion point where linked file will be inserted.

   OR

   Place insertion point anywhere in linked spreadsheet to edit.

2. Select <u>T</u>ools menu .... **Alt**+**T**

3. Select Spr<u>e</u>adsheet .... **E**

4. Select <u>C</u>reate Link .... **C**

   OR   **OR**

   Select <u>E</u>dit Link .... **E**

5. If necessary, type or edit filename of spreadsheet
   to link in <u>F</u>ilename text box .... **filename**

   NOTE: If necessary, type path to file.
   Example: C:\123\123191.WKS

   OR   **OR**

   Open <u>F</u>ilename 🔽 **F4**
   <u>and</u> select filename (pages 25, 26).

   To limit link to a range in spreadsheet:

   a) Select <u>R</u>ange text box .... **Alt**+**R**

   b) Type range of cells .... **range**
      Example: A1:B20

   OR   **OR**

   Select a range name in
   Range <u>N</u>ame list box .... **Alt**+**N**, **↕**

6. Select ○ <u>T</u>able .... **Alt**+**T**

   OR   **OR**

   Select ○ Te<u>x</u>t .... **Alt**+**X**

7. Select **OK** .... **↵**

Comment codes mark beginning and end of linked data.

234

Update All Spreadsheet Links

1. Select **T**ools menu .... **Alt** + **T**
2. Select Spr**e**adsheet .... **E**
3. Select **U**pdate All Links .... **U**
4. Select **Y**es .... **↵**

Update Single Spreadsheet Link

1. Place insertion point anywhere in linked spreadsheet.
2. Select **T**ools menu .... **Alt** + **T**
3. Select Spr**e**adsheet .... **E**
4. Select **E**dit Link .... **E**
5. Select **OK** .... **↵**

Linked Spreadsheet Options

1. Select **T**ools menu .... **Alt** + **T**
2. Select Spr**e**adsheet .... **E**
3. Select **L**ink Options .... **L**
4. Select or clear desired options:

   ☐ **U**pdate Links on Document Open .... **U**
   Select to automatically update all links when you open the document.

   ☐ **S**how Link Codes .... **S**
   Select to display beginning and ending link comments.

5. Select **OK** to return to document .... **↵**

Delete Spreadsheet Link without Deleting Data

1. If necessary, turn Reveal Codes on .... **Alt** + **F3**
2. Highlight desired [Link:...] or [Link End] code.
3. Press **Delete** .... **Del**

STYLES

Use styles to quickly and consistently format your document. Using styles also makes it very easy to change the look of your document in one step by simply changing the codes the style contains.

Create a Style

When you create a style, it is saved with current document only. To save a style for use with other documents, see page 237.

1. Select Layout menu .... `Alt`+`L`
2. Select Styles .... `S`
3. Select Create .... `Alt`+`C`
4. Type name of style in Name text box .... **name**
5. Select Description text box .... `Tab`
6. Type style description .... **text**
7. Open Type `[____ ÷]` .... `Alt`+`T`, `F4`
   and select desired style type:

   • Open .... `O`
     Select an Open style when the codes in the style will remain in effect until another style or code is encountered. (Like a Margin code.)

   • Paired .... `P`
     Select a Paired style when the codes in the style will only affect text between the style's On and Off codes. (Like Underline codes.)
     If Paired was selected,

     • Open Enter Key Inserts `[____ ÷]` .. `Alt`+`E`, `F4`
       and select desired Enter key option:

       • Hard Return .... `H`
         to insert a hard return when **Enter** is pressed.

       • Style Off .... `F`
         to turn style off and insert a hard return when **Enter** is pressed.

       • Style Off/On .... `O`
         to turn style off, insert a hard return and turn style on again when **Enter** is pressed again.

Continued ...

STYLES — Create a Style (continued)

8. Select **OK** . . . . ⏎

FROM STYLE EDITOR

9. If creating a paired style, place insertion point above or below comment as described in comment.

10. Type text an/or insert format codes to include in style.

11. Repeat steps 9 and 10 as needed.

   To change properties of style from Style Editor:

   a) Select Properties . . . . `Alt`+`P`

   b) Make desired changes (steps 4-7, previous page).

   c) Select **OK** . . . . ⏎

12. Select **C**lose . . . . `Alt`+`C`

13. Select **O**n to turn style on in document . . . . . . `Alt`+`O`

   OR   **OR**

   Select **Close** to return to document . . . . `Alt`+`F4`

Edit Style

Changes to a style will affect every occurrence of text to which you have applied the style in the current document.

1. Select **L**ayout menu . . . . `Alt`+`L`

2. Select **S**tyles . . . . `S`

3. Select style to edit in list box . . . . `¼`

4. Select **E**dit . . . . `Alt`+`E`

FROM STYLE EDITOR

5. Insert and delete text and/or codes as desired.

   To change properties of style from Style Editor:

   a) Select Properties . . . . `Alt`+`P`

   b) Make desired changes.
      See Create a Style, steps 4-7 on page 235.

   c) Select **OK** . . . . ⏎

6. Select **C**lose . . . . `Alt`+`C`

7. Select **Close** to return to document . . . . `Alt`+`F4`

STYLES (continued)

Turn Style On

1. If inserting an open style, place insertion point where style format will begin.

   OR

   Select text (page 218) to which paired style will be applied.

2. Select **L**ayout menu .... **Alt** + **L**
3. Select **S**tyles .... **S**
4. Select desired style in list box .... **↑⁄↓**
5. Select **O**n .... **↵**

End Paired Style in Document

1. Place insertion point within paired style codes where style will end.
2. Select **L**ayout menu .... **Alt** + **L**
3. Select **S**tyle .... **S**
4. Select O**ff** .... **↵**

OR   **OR**

1. If necessary, turn Reveal Codes on .... **Alt** + **F3**
2. Move highlight before a [Style On: name...] code, or after a [Style Off: name...] code.

Save Styles for Use in Other Documents

1. Select **L**ayout menu .... **Alt** + **L**
2. Select **S**tyles .... **S**
3. Select **S**ave As .... **Alt** + **S**
4. Type a filename for styles .... **filename**
5. Select **S**ave .... **↵**
6. Select **Close** .... **↵**

STYLES (continued)

Retrieve Styles Into Current Document

1. Select **L**ayout menu .... `Alt`+`L`
2. Select **S**tyles .... `S`
3. Select **R**etrieve .... `Alt`+`R`
4. Select filename of style in F**i**les list box .. `Alt`+`I`, `↕`
   See DIRECTORIES — LOCATING FILES on page 25.

   If "Style(s) Already Exist. Replace ?" message appears,

   - Select **Y**es .... `↵`
     to replace existing styles with same name
     with style codes from incoming file.

   OR   **OR**

     Select **N**o .... `N`
     to retain contents of existing style names.

5. Select **Close** .... `↵`

Delete a Style Code in Document

Also see Delete Style Throughout Document on next page.

- Delete desired [Style On: name...], [Style Off: name...]
  or [Open Style: name...] style code.
  (See DELETE CODES on page 23.)

STYLES (continued)

Delete Style Throughout Document

1. Select **L**ayout menu .... `Alt`+`L`
2. Select **S**tyles .... `S`
3. Select style to delete in list box .... `⇵`
4. Select **D**elete .... `Alt`+`D`
5. Select one option:

   ○ **L**eave Format Codes .... `L`
   Deletes style from Styles dialog box and all style codes with same name from document, and converts the style's format codes to standard format codes.

   ○ **D**elete Format Codes .... `D`
   Deletes style from Styles dialog box and all style codes with same name from document.

   ○ Delete Definition **O**nly .... `O`
   Deletes style from Styles dialog box and leaves style codes in document.

6. Select **OK** .... `⏎`
7. Select **Close** to return to document .... `⏎`

SUPPRESS

Prevents a page number, header, or footer from appearing on a particular page. You can also use Suppress to print current page number at bottom center of page.

1. Place insertion point at top of page.
2. Select **L**ayout menu .... `Alt`+`L`
3. Select **P**age .... `P`
4. Select S**u**ppress .... `U`
5. Select item(s) to suppress .... **letter**
   Header A, H**e**ader B, **F**ooter A, Fo**o**ter B, **P**age Numbers,

   To print current page number at bottom center of page:

   • Select ☐Print Page **N**umber at Bottom Center `Alt`+`N`

6. Select **OK** .... `⏎`

TAB

With the tab feature you can set tab stops at specified positions in your document. You can then use the Tab and Indent keys as well as other alignment commands to vertically align text on these tab stops.

Set Tabs

Also see Change Tab Setting using the Ruler on page 208.

1. Place insertion point where tab settings will begin.

2. Select **L**ayout menu . . . . **Alt** + **L**

3. Select **L**ine . . . . **L**

4. Select **T**ab Set . . . . **T**

5. Select ○ Left **E**dge (Abs) . . . . **Alt** + **E**
   to set tabs stops measured <u>from left edge</u> of page.

   OR   **OR**

   Select ○ Left **M**argin (Rel) . . . . **Alt** + **M**
   to set tabs stops <u>relative to left margin</u>.

   To <u>clear all</u> tab stops:

   • Select Clear Ta**b**s . . . . **Alt** + **B**

   To <u>clear individual</u> tab stops:

   a) Select tab stop number to clear
      in **P**osition list box . . . . **Alt** + **P**, **⇅**

   b) Select Clear T**a**b . . . . **Alt** + **A**

   c) Repeat steps a and b for each tab stop to clear.

   To set <u>evenly spaced</u> tab stops:

   a) Select Clear Ta**b**s . . . . **Alt** + **B**

   b) Select ☐ E**v**enly Spaced . . . . **Alt** + **V**

   c) Type starting position in **P**osition text box . . . . **number**

   d) Select Repea**t** Every text box . . . . **Alt** + **T**

   e) Type interval between tab stops (inches) . . . . . **number**

   f) Select **S**et Tab . . . . **Alt** + **S**

Continued ...

TAB — Set Tabs (continued)

To <u>create individual</u> tab stops:

a) If desired, clear existing tab stops (previous page).

b) Select <u>P</u>osition text box . . . . **Alt** + **P**

c) Type tab position . . . . **number**

d) Select desired tab type . . . . **Alt** + **letter**
<u>L</u>eft Align, <u>C</u>enter, <u>R</u>ight Align, <u>D</u>ecimal Align

   To create a dot leader tab stop:

   • Select ☐D<u>o</u>t Leader Tabs . . . . **Alt** + **O**

e) Select <u>S</u>et Tab . . . . **Alt** + **S**

f) Repeat steps c-e for each tab stop to set.

To <u>change type</u> of existing tab:

a) Select tab stop number to change
in <u>P</u>osition list box . . . . **Alt** + **P**, **↑/↓**

b) Select desired tab type . . . . **Alt** + **letter**
<u>L</u>eft Align, <u>C</u>enter, <u>R</u>ight Align, <u>D</u>ecimal Align

   To create a dot leader tab stop:

   • Select ☐D<u>o</u>t Leader Tabs . . . . **Alt** + **O**

c) Select <u>S</u>et Tab . . . . **Alt** + **S**

To return tab stops to <u>default setting</u>:

• Select De<u>f</u>ault . . . . **Alt** + **F**

   NOTE: *By default, the tab settings have been set
   to one tab stop every .5 inches.*

6. Select **OK** . . . . **↵**

Examples of tab types:

Tab Type	Example	Tab Type	Example
Left Align	The Dog	Right Align with dot leader	The . . . . . Dog
Center	The Dog	Decimal Align	22.42 113.63

242

Change Decimal Align Character

*Sets character on which vertical alignment will occur when you press Decimal Tab Align — **Ctrl + F6** (DOS 5.1) or **Alt + Shift + F7** (CUA). By default, the decimal tab align character is a period.*

1. Place insertion point where new alignment setting will begin.
2. Select **L**ayout menu .... `Alt`+`L`
3. Select **L**ine .... `L`
4. Select Special C**o**des .... `O`
5. Select ○Decimal Align Character .... `G`
6. Select text box .... `Tab`
7. Type new alignment character .... **character**
8. Select **I**nsert .... `⏎`

TABLE OF AUTHORITIES

A Table of Authorities is a list of citations used primarily in legal documents. It lists where citations of specific cases and statutes appear in the document.

There are three basic steps for creating a table of authorities:

* *Define table sections (next page).*
* *Mark text (citations) in document to include in table (page 244).*
* *Generate the table (page 90).*

TABLE OF AUTHORITIES (continued)

Define Table of Authority Sections

You can create up to 16 sections. Some of most commonly used sections are: Cases, Constitutional Provisions, Regulatory Provisions, Statutory Provisions, and Miscellaneous.

1. On a separate page where table will be generated, type heading for table, then type section names and separate each with a blank line as shown in example below.

2. Place insertion point below section name to define.

3. Select <u>T</u>ools menu . . . . `Alt`+`T`

4. Select De<u>f</u>ine . . . . `F`

5. Select Table of <u>A</u>uthorities . . . . `A`

6. Type number of section (1-16) in Section <u>N</u>umber increment box to define . . . . **number**

7. Select desired format(s) for section:

   ☐ <u>D</u>ot Leaders . . . . `Alt`+`D`

   ☐ <u>U</u>nderlining Allowed . . . . `Alt`+`U`

   ☐ <u>B</u>lank Line Between Authorities . . . . `Alt`+`B`

8. Select **OK** . . . . `↵`

9. Repeat steps 2-8 for each section to define.

   If your table is at the beginning of the document,

   a) Insert a hard page below the table . . . . `Ctrl`+`↵`

   b) Insert a new page number (page 175) at the top of your first page of text.

Example:

                    TABLE OF AUTHORITIES

        Cases

        Statutes

        ==================================
                        page 1

244

Mark <u>First Occurrence</u> of a Citation for Table of Authorities — Full Form

1. Select text (citation) that will be included in table.
2. Select <u>T</u>ools menu . . . . **Alt** + **T**
3. Select Mar**k** Text . . . . **K**
4. Select ToA <u>F</u>ull Form . . . . **F**
5. Type number of section the citation belongs to . . **number**
6. Select Short <u>F</u>orm text box . . . . **Tab**
7. Type a unique Short Form name for citation . . . . **text**
8. Select **OK** . . . . **↵**

FROM TABLE OF AUTHORITIES FULL FORM EDITOR

9. Edit and format text to specify how it will appear in table.
10. Select <u>C</u>lose to return to document . . . . **Alt** + **C**
11. Repeat steps 1-10 for each first occurrence of a citation.

Mark <u>Subsequent Occurrences</u> of a Citation for Table of Authorities — Short Form

1. Search (page 213) for next citation for which a Short Form name has been defined (see above).
2. Place insertion point after citation to mark.
3. Select <u>T</u>ools menu . . . . **Alt** + **T**
4. Select Mar**k** Text . . . . **K**
5. Select ToA <u>S</u>hort Form . . . . **S**
6. Edit or accept proposed short form name . . . . **text**
7. Select **OK** . . . . **↵**
8. Repeat steps 1-7 for each citation for which a Short Form name has been defined.

Generate Table of Authorities

See GENERATE on page 90.

TABLE OF CONTENTS

There are three basic steps for creating a table of contents:

- *Mark text to include in the table.*
- *Define the location and numbering format for each level.*
- *Generate the table.*

Mark Text for Table of Contents

1. Select text (page 218) to include in table of contents.
2. Select **T**ools menu .... `Alt` + `T`
3. Select Mar**k** Text .... `K`
4. Select Table of **C**ontents .... `C`
5. Type topic level (1-5) .... **number**
6. Select **OK** .... `⏎`
7. Repeat steps 1-6 for each item to mark.

Define Location and Format for Table of Contents

1. If desired, change page numbering style (page 174).

   NOTE: *The Page Format command provides for Arabic or Roman numbering, as well as accompanying text (such as Lesson One, Page ^B). Note that the format you choose for numbering will also affect the text in your document.*

2. On a separate page where table will be generated, type heading for table then press **Enter**.

   If table of contents is located at beginning of document,

   a) Insert a hard page .... `Ctrl` + `⏎`
      to separate table of contents from text in document.

   b) Insert a new page number (page 175) at top of page where document begins.

   c) Place insertion point on page below heading for table of contents.

3. Select **T**ools menu .... `Alt` + `T`
4. Select De**f**ine .... `F`

Continued ...

TABLE OF CONTENTS (continued)

5. Select Table of <u>C</u>ontents . . . . `C`

6. Type number (1-5) of levels to include in table . . . **number**

7. Open Level # `[____ ◆]` . . . . `Alt` + `F`, `F4`
   <u>and</u> select desired number style:

   - <u>N</u>o Numbering . . . . `N`

   - Text <u>#</u> . . . . `#`
     Text and page number is separated by a space.

   - <u>T</u>ext (#) . . . . `T`
     Text and page number in parenthesis separated
     by a space.

   - T<u>e</u>xt   # . . . . `E`
     Text followed by a flush right page number.

   - Te<u>x</u>t....# . . . . `X`
     Text followed by a flush right page number
     with dot leaders.

   To align text in table evenly when it wraps to next line:

   - Select ☐<u>L</u>ast Level in Wrapped Format . . . . `Alt` + `L`

8. Repeat steps 6 and 7 for each number level to format.

9. Select **OK** . . . . `↵`

Generate Table of Contents

See GENERATE on page 90.

TABLES

Create a Table

Also see Create Tables using the Ruler on page 210.

1. Select **L**ayout menu .... `Alt` + `L`
2. Select **T**ables .... `T`
3. Select **C**reate .... `C`
4. Type number of columns in **C**olumns text box .... **number**
5. Select **R**ows text box .... `Tab`
6. Type number of rows .... **number**
7. Select OK .... `⏎`

Insertion Point Movement in Tables

Next cell .... `Tab`

Previous cell .... `Shift` + `Tab`

First cell in row (CUA) .... `Home`, `Home`

Last cell in row .... `End`, `End`

Up or Down one cell .... `Alt` + `↕`

Previous or Next column .... `Alt` + `↔`

Top line of cell (CUA) .... `Alt` + `Home`

Bottom line of cell (CUA) .... `Alt` + `End`

TABLES (continued)

Select Cells using Mouse

When cells are selected, the text in the cells is also selected and you can use table structure or table format settings. To select only the text within a table, see Select Text (page 218).

Select one cell:

a) Point to <u>top</u> or <u>left border</u> of cell to select.
   Pointer becomes a ⇧ *or* ⇦.

b) Click mouse button.

Select all cells in a column:

a) Point to <u>top border</u> of any cell in column.
   Pointer becomes a ⇧.

b) Double-click mouse button.

Select all cells in a row:

a) Point to <u>left border</u> of any cell in row.
   Pointer becomes a ⇦.

b) Double-click mouse button.

Select all cells in a table:

a) Point to <u>top</u> or <u>left border</u> of any cell.
   Pointer becomes a ⇧ *or* ⇦.

b) Triple-click mouse button.

Deselect all cells in a table:

• Click in any cell.

TABLES (continued)

Select Cells using Keyboard

1. Place insertion point in first cell to select.
2. Press **Shift + F8** (CUA) . . . . `Shift` + `F8`

   OR   **OR**

   Press **Shift + F12** (WP 5.1 DOS) . . . . `Shift` + `F12`
   First cell is selected.

   To extend selection:

   one cell in any direction . . . . `Shift` + `↕`

   to beginning of row (CUA only) . . . . `Shift` + `Home`

   to end of row . . . . `Shift` + `End`

   to include current row . . . . `Ctrl` + `↕`

   to include current column . . . . `Ctrl` + `↔`

   to include entire table . . . . `Ctrl` + `↑`, `Ctrl` + `→`

   To deselect extended selection:

   • Repeat step 2.

Insert Rows/Columns in Table

1. Place insertion point in table where rows or
   columns will be inserted.
2. Select **L**ayout menu . . . . `Alt` + `L`
3. Select **T**ables . . . . `T`
4. Select **I**nsert . . . . `I`
5. Select ○ **C**olumns . . . . `Alt` + `C`

   OR   **OR**

   Select ○ **R**ows . . . . `Alt` + `R`
6. Select text box . . . . `Tab`
7. Type number of columns or rows . . . . **number**
8. Select **OK** . . . . `↵`

NOTE: To quickly insert one row, press Alt + Ins.
To quickly delete current row, press Alt + Del.

250

Change Number of Rows and Columns in Table

Adds or deletes rows from bottom of the table or adds and deletes columns from the right side of table. Also see Delete Row/Column (Structure and Text) on page 251 and Delete Rows/Columns (Structure or Text) on page 252.

1. Place insertion point in table.
2. Select Layout menu .... `Alt`+`L`
3. Select Tables .... `T`
4. Select Options .... `O`

   To change number of columns in table:
   - Type number of columns in Columns text box . **number**

   To change number of rows in table:
   a) Select Rows text box .... `Tab`
   b) Type number of rows .... **number**
5. Select OK .... `↵`

Format Table Lines

1. Place insertion point in cell to format.
   OR
   Select cells (pages 248, 249) to format.
2. Select Layout menu .... `Alt`+`L`
3. Select Tables .... `T`
4. Select Lines .... `L`
5. Open desired line's `☐ ⬍` .... `Alt`+letter, `F4`
   and select a line type .... **letter**
   None, Single, Double, Dashed, Dotted, Thick, Extra Thick, Mixed
6. Repeat step 5 for each line to format.
7. Select OK .... `↵`

TABLES (continued)

Delete Table

Deletes entire table (structure and text), only the table structure, or only the table text.

1. Select all cells in table (pages 248, 249).

2. Press **Delete** .... `Del`

3. Select one option:

   ○ **E**ntire Table (structure and text) .... `E`

   ○ **C**ontents (text only) .... `C`

   ○ **T**able Structure (leaves text) .... `T`

4. Select **OK** .... `↵`

Delete Row/Column (Structure and Text)

Also see Delete Rows/Columns (Structure or Text) on next page.

1. Place insertion point in first row or column to delete.

2. Select **L**ayout menu .... `Alt`+`L`

3. Select **T**ables .... `T`

4. Select **D**elete .... `D`

5. Select ○ **C**olumns .... `C`

   OR   **OR**

   Select ○ **R**ows .... `R`

6. Select text box .... `Tab`

7. Type number of columns or rows to delete ...... **number**

8. Select **OK** .... `↵`

Delete Rows/Columns (Structure or Text)

1. Select all cells in rows or columns to delete (pages 248, 249).

2. Press **Delete** .... `Del`

   To delete <u>structure and text of row</u>:

   • Select ○ **R**ows(s) .... `R`

   To delete <u>structure and text of column</u>:

   Select ○ **C**olumn(s) .... `C`

   To delete <u>only the text</u>:

   • Select ○ C**o**ntents (text only) .... `O`

3. Select **OK** .... `↵`

Convert Tabular or Parallel Columns to a Table

1. Select text (page 218) in columns to convert.

2. Select **L**ayout menu .... `Alt`+`L`

3. Select **T**ables .... `T`

4. Select **C**reate .... `C`

   If selected text columns are tabular,

   • Select ○ **T**abular Column .... `T`

   If selected text columns are parallel,

   • Select ○ **P**arallel Column .... `P`

5. Select **OK** .... `↵`

TABLES (continued)

Adjust Horizontal Table Position

Also see Adjust Table Margins using the Ruler on page 211.

1. Place insertion point in table.
2. Select **L**ayout menu .... `Alt`+`L`
3. Select **T**ables .... `T`
4. Select **O**ptions .... `O`
5. Select desired table position:

   ○ **L**eft (left justify table) .... `Alt`+`L`

   ○ **R**ight (right justify table) .... `Alt`+`I`

   ○ Ce**n**ter (center table within margins) .... `Alt`+`N`

   ○ **F**ull (force table to fill space
   between margins) .... `Alt`+`F`

   ○ Fr**o**m Left Edge (place table a specific
   distance from left edge of page) .... `Alt`+`O`

      a) Select text box .... `Tab`

      b) Type distance (inches) from
         left edge of page .... **number**

6. Select **OK** .... `↵`

Change Cell Margins

Defines space between text and cell borders for entire table.

1. Place insertion point within table to format.
2. Select **L**ayout menu .... `Alt`+`L`
3. Select **T**ables .... `T`
4. Select **O**ptions .... `O`
5. Select desired cell margins text box .... `Alt`+letter
   Left, Right, Top, Bottom
6. Type margin (inches) .... **number**
7. Repeat steps 5 and 6 for each margin to change.
8. Select **OK** .... `↵`

TABLES (continued)

Set Percent of Shading for Cells

This procedure sets the percentage of grey when cells are shaded.
It does not turn shading on. See topic that follows.

1. Place insertion point in table.
2. Select **L**ayout menu .... **Alt**+**L**
3. Select **T**ables .... **T**
4. Select **O**ptions .... **O**
5. Select **S**hading Percent increment box .... **Alt**+**S**
6. Type percentage (0-100) .... **number**
   Where 100 is black and 0 is white.
7. Select **OK** .... ↵

Shade Cells in a Table

Shades cells a shade of grey as specified in topic above. It is not possible
to use different shades in a table.

1. Place insertion point within cell to shade.

   OR

   Select cells (pages 248, 249) to shade.
2. Select **L**ayout menu .... **Alt**+**L**
3. Select **T**ables .... **T**
4. Select C**e**ll .... **E**
5. Select □S**h**ading .... **Alt**+**H**
6. Select **OK** .... ↵

TABLES (continued)

Join Cells

Combines two or more cells into one cell.

1. Select cells (pages 248, 249) to join.
2. Select **L**ayout menu .... `Alt`+`L`
3. Select **T**ables .... `T`
4. Select **J**oin .... `J`

Split Cell into Multiple Rows or Columns

1. Place insertion point in cell to split.

   OR

   Select cells (pages 248, 249) to split.
2. Select **L**ayout menu .... `Alt`+`L`
3. Select **T**ables .... `T`
4. Select **S**plit .... `S`
5. Select ○ **C**olumn .... `C`

   OR   **OR**

   Select ○ **R**ow .... `R`
6. Select text box .... `Tab`
7. Type number of columns or rows to create ..... **number**
8. Select **OK** .... `↵`

256

Cell Text — Size/Appearance

Automatically formats the size and appearance of text in specified cells. Also see Table Column Text — Size/Appearance on next page.

1. Place insertion point in cell to format.

   OR

   Select cells (pages 248, 249) to format.

2. Select **L**ayout menu .... `Alt`+`L`

3. Select **T**ables .... `T`

4. Select C**e**ll .... `E`

   To change <u>text appearance</u> in cells:

   - Select or clear appearance options .... **letter**
     ***B**old, **U**nderline, **D**ouble Underline, **I**talic, **O**utline, Shado**w**, Small **C**ap, **R**edline, Stri**k**eout*

   To change <u>size of text</u> in cells:

   - Select or clear size options .... **letter**
     *Su**p**erscript, Subscrip**t**, **F**ine, **S**mall, **L**arge, **V**ery Large, **E**xtra Large*

   To use column size and appearance in cells:

   - Select ☐Use Column Si**z**e and Appearance ...... `Z`
     NOTE: Select to override cell settings and use column appearance and size settings. See Table Column Text — Size/Appearance on next page.

5. Select **OK** .... `↵`

TABLES (continued)

Table Column Text — Size/Appearance

Automatically formats the size and appearance of text in specified columns. Also see Cell Text — Size/Appearance on previous page.

1. Place insertion point in any cell in column to format.

   OR

   Select columns in table (pages 248, 249) to format.

2. Select **L**ayout menu .... **Alt** + **L**

3. Select **T**ables .... **T**

4. Select Col**u**mn .... **U**

   To change <u>text appearance</u> in columns:

   - Select or clear appearance options .... **letter**
     *Bold, <u>U</u>nderline, <u>D</u>ouble Underline, <u>I</u>talic, Outline,
     Shado<u>w</u>, Small <u>C</u>ap, <u>R</u>edline, Stri<u>k</u>eout*

   To change <u>size of text</u> in columns:

   - Select or clear size options .... **letter**
     *Su<u>p</u>erscript, Subscript, <u>F</u>ine, <u>S</u>mall, <u>L</u>arge,
     <u>V</u>ery Large, <u>E</u>xtra Large*

5. Select **OK** .... **↵**

Vertically Align Text in Cells

1. Place insertion point in cell to format.

   OR

   Select cells (pages 248, 249) to format.

2. Select **L**ayout menu .... **Alt** + **L**

3. Select **T**ables .... **T**

4. Select C**e**ll .... **E**

5. Open **A**lignment [＿＿ ♦] .... **A**, **F4**

   and select desired option .... **letter**
   <u>T</u>op, <u>B</u>ottom, <u>C</u>enter, <u>M</u>ixed

6. Select **OK** .... **↵**

NOTE: *You must print (page 184) or preview (page 188) the document to see the new alignment.*

TABLES (continued)

Lock or Unlock Cells

Lock cells to prevent text in cells from being altered.
Also see Disable/Enable Cell Locking below.

1. Place insertion point in cell to lock or unlock.

   OR

   Select cells (pages 248, 249) to lock or unlock.

2. Select Layout menu .... `Alt`+`L`
3. Select Tables .... `T`
4. Select Cell .... `E`
5. Select or clear □Lock .... `O`
6. Select OK .... `⏎`

Disable/Enable Cell Locking

1. Place insertion point in table that contains locked cells.
2. Select Layout menu .... `Alt`+`L`
3. Select Tables .... `T`
4. Select Options .... `O`
5. Select or clear □Disable Cell Locks .... `Alt`+`D`
6. Select OK .... `⏎`

TABLES (continued)

Justify Text in Cells

1. Place insertion point in cell to format.

   OR

   Select cells (pages 248, 249) to format.

2. Select <u>L</u>ayout menu .... `Alt`+`L`
3. Select <u>T</u>ables .... `T`
4. Select C<u>e</u>ll .... `E`
5. Open <u>J</u>ustification [_____ ⬍] .... `J`, `F4`

   <u>an</u>d select desired alignment .... **letter**

   <u>L</u>eft, <u>F</u>ull, <u>C</u>enter, <u>R</u>ight, <u>D</u>ecimal Align, <u>M</u>ixed

   To use column justification in cells:

   • Select ☐Use Colu<u>m</u>n Justification .... `M`

     NOTE: *Select to override cell justification and use*
     column column justification. See Justify Text
     in Table Columns below.

6. Select **OK** .... `↵`

Justify Text in Table Columns

1. Place insertion point in column to format.

   OR

   Select columns (pages 248, 249) to format.

2. Select <u>L</u>ayout menu .... `Alt`+`L`
3. Select <u>T</u>ables .... `T`
4. Select Col<u>u</u>mn .... `U`
5. Open <u>J</u>ustification [_____ ⬍] .... `J`, `F4`

   <u>an</u>d select desired alignment .... **letter**

   <u>L</u>eft, <u>F</u>ull, <u>C</u>enter, <u>R</u>ight, <u>D</u>ecimal Align, <u>M</u>ixed

6. Select **OK** .... `↵`

TABLES (continued)

Table Headers

Sets a specified number of rows in a table, beginning with row one, to repeat at the top of each subsequent page if a table continues on multiple pages.

1. Place insertion point in table.
2. Select **L**ayout menu .... `Alt`+`L`
3. Select **T**ables .... `T`
4. Select **O**ptions .... `O`
5. Select **A**ttributes Header Rows text box .... `Alt`+`A`
6. Type number of header rows .... **number**
7. Select **OK** .... `↵`

NOTE: *You must print (page 184) or preview (page 188) the document to see the headers on subsequent pages.*

Adjust Column Width in Table

Also see Adjust Table Columns using the Ruler on page 211.

1. Place insertion point in column to adjust.

   OR

   Select columns (pages 248, 249) to adjust.
2. Select **L**ayout menu .... `Alt`+`L`
3. Select **T**ables .... `T`
4. Select Col**u**mn .... `U`
5. Select C**o**lumn Width text box .... `O`
6. Type width of column (inches) .... **number**
7. Select **OK** .... `↵`

TABLES (continued)

Adjust Row Height in Table

1. Place insertion point in row to adjust.

   OR

   Select rows (pages 248, 249) to adjust.

2. Select <u>L</u>ayout menu .... <kbd>Alt</kbd> + <kbd>L</kbd>

3. Select <u>T</u>ables .... <kbd>T</kbd>

4. Select <u>R</u>ow .... <kbd>R</kbd>

   To set row for single or multiple lines:

   • Select ○<u>S</u>ingle Line .... <kbd>S</kbd>
     Sets row to accept only a single line of text.
     OR   **OR**

   Select ○<u>M</u>ulti Line (default setting) .... <kbd>M</kbd>
   Sets row so that its height will adjust as text wraps in cell.

   To set row to a fixed or self-adjusting height:

   • Select ○<u>A</u>uto (default setting) .... <kbd>A</kbd>
     Sets row to adjust to largest font in row.
     OR   **OR**

   Select ○<u>F</u>ixed .... <kbd>F</kbd>
   Sets row height to a specific size.

   If <u>F</u>ixed was selected,

   a) Select text box .... <kbd>Tab</kbd>

   b) Type row height .... **number**

5. Select **OK** .... <kbd>↵</kbd>

TABLES (continued)

Create or Edit Formula in Table

Use formulas in table cells to calculate values in other cells.
Also see Recalculate a Table Formula below.

1. Place insertion point in cell that will receive formula
   or contains formula to edit.

2. Select **L**ayout menu . . . . **Alt**+**L**

3. Select **T**ables . . . . **T**

4. Select **F**ormula . . . . **F**

5. Type or edit formula or function
   in **F**ormula text box . . . . **formula**

   NOTE: *Formulas can include numbers, operators (+ - * /),*
   and cell addresses (such as A1). Functions (+ = *)
   are used alone to find subtotals, totals, and
   grandtotals (see examples below).

   Examples of a formula and functions:

   (A1+B1)/C1 totals contents of cells A1 and B1, then divides the sum
   by contents of cell C1.

   + (Subtotal function) adds all numbers directly above the function.

   = (Total function) adds subtotals above the function.

   * (Grand Total function) adds totals above the function.

6. Select **OK** . . . . **↵**

Recalculate a Table Formula

Recalculates cells referenced by table formulas and displays results.

1. Place insertion point in table to recalculate.

2. Select **L**ayout menu . . . . **Alt**+**L**

3. Select **T**ables . . . . **T**

4. Select C**a**lculate . . . . **A**

NOTE: *If WordPerfect cannot calculate formula (i.e., the formula is*
incorrect), it displays a double question mark (??) in cell.

TABLES (continued)

Delete a Table Formula

1. Select cell or cells (pages 248, 249) that contains formula(s) to delete.

2. Press **Delete** .... `Del`

Copy a Table Formula

1. Place insertion point in cell that contains formula to copy.

2. Select **L**ayout menu .... `Alt`+`L`

3. Select **T**ables .... `T`

4. Select **F**ormula .... `F`

   To copy formula to a specific cell:

   a) Select ○ **T**o Cell .... `Alt`+`T`

   b) Select text box .... `Tab`

   c) Type address of cell to receive formula ... **cell address**

   To copy formula down a specified number of times:

   a) Select ○ **D**own .... `Alt`+`D`

   b) Select text box .... `Tab`

   c) Type number of times to copy formula ...... **number**

   To copy formula right a specified number of times:

   a) Select ○ **R**ight .... `Alt`+`R`

   b) Select text box .... `Tab`

   c) Type number of times to copy formula ...... **number**

5. Select **OK** .... `↵`

264

Ignore Cell During Calculations

1. Place insertion point in cell to ignore.

   OR

   Select cells (pages 248, 249) to ignore.

2. Select <u>L</u>ayout menu . . . . `Alt`+`L`

3. Select <u>T</u>ables . . . . `T`

4. Select C<u>e</u>ll . . . . `E`

5. Select ☐I<u>g</u>nore Cell When Calculating . . . . `G`

6. Select **OK** . . . . `↵`

7. Recalculate table formulas (page 262).

Specify Format of Negative Calculation Results

1. Place insertion point in table.

2. Select <u>L</u>ayout menu . . . . `Alt`+`L`

3. Select <u>T</u>ables . . . . `T`

4. Select <u>O</u>ptions . . . . `O`

5. Select <u>M</u>inus Sign -22 . . . . `Alt`+`M`

   OR   **OR**

   Select <u>P</u>arentheses (22) . . . . `Alt`+`P`

6. Select **OK** . . . . `↵`

Specify Decimal Places to Display in Formula Result

1. Place insertion point in column containing formula.

2. Select <u>L</u>ayout menu . . . . `Alt`+`L`

3. Select <u>T</u>ables . . . . `T`

4. Select Col<u>u</u>mn . . . . `U`

5. Select Di<u>g</u>its text box . . . . `G`

6. Type number of decimal digits (1-15) to calculate . **number**

7. Select **OK** . . . . `↵`

TEXT COLOR

Determines color of text on screen and in printed document.

NOTE: *You must deselect the "Text in Windows System Colors"*
option (page 29) to show colors on screen as selected
in the steps that follow.

Change Text to a Predefined Color

1. Place insertion point where color change will begin.

   OR

   Select text (page 218) to format.

2. Select F**o**nt menu . . . . `Alt`+`O`

3. Select **C**olor . . . . `C`

4. Open **P**redefined Colors [⬚ ⬍] . . . . . . `Alt`+`P`, `F4`

   and select desired color . . . . **letter**

   Black, **W**hite, **R**ed, Gr**e**en, B**l**ue, **Y**ellow, **M**agenta, Cy**a**n,
   Orange, **G**ray, Brow**n**

5. Select **OK** . . . . `↵`

   If text was selected,

   • Press **Right** arrow to deselect text . . . . `→`

   If text was not selected,

   a) Type text . . . . **text**

   b) Repeat steps 2-5 to change text color.

266

TEXT COLOR (continued)

Change Text to a Custom Color

NOTE: *Your printer may not support custom colors.*

1. Place insertion point where color change will begin.

   OR

   Select text (page 218) to format.

2. Select F**o**nt menu . . . . **Alt**+**O**

3. Select **C**olor . . . . **C**

4. a) Drag ■ on lumination bar until desired color intensity appears in color wheel.

   b) Drag ■ on color wheel to desired color.

   c) Repeat steps a and b until desired color appears.

   OR

   a) Select desired color option text box . . . . . . **Alt**+**letter**

      R*ed,* ***G****reen,* ***B****lue,* ***H****ue,* ***S****aturation,* ***L****umination*

Hue	Adjusts the ratio of Red, Green and Blue.
Lumination	Adjusts the lightness or darkness of the Hue, where 0 is black and 100 is white.
Saturation	Adjusts the purity of the Hue, where 0 is diluted and 100 is a pure color.

   b) Press **Up** and **Down** arrows
      until desired color appears . . . . ↑↓

   c) Repeat steps a and b until desired color appears.

5. Select **OK** . . . . ↵

   If text was selected,

   • Press **Right** arrow to deselect text . . . . →

   If text was <u>not</u> selected,

   a) Type text . . . . **text**

   b) Repeat steps 2-5 to change text color.

THESAURUS

Displays synonyms (words with same meaning) and antonyms (words with opposite meaning) for a specified word and gives the option to replace the word or look up additional synonyms and antonyms.

Look Up Synonym or Antonym of Word

1. Place insertion point anywhere on word.

2. Select **T**ools menu . . . . **Alt**+**T**

3. Select **T**hesaurus . . . . **T**
   WordPerfect display words found in its dictionary.
   To show related words:
   NOTE: Only words with bullets contain related words.

   • Double-click on any word marked with a bullet.

   OR

   a) Select word marked with a bullet in list box   **Tab**, **↑↓**
      If necessary, press Tab until list box is selected.

   b) Press **Enter** . . . . **↵**
   WordPerfect displays related words in next list box.
   To look up a word:

   a) Select **W**ord text box . . . . **Alt**+**W**

   b) Type word . . . . **text**

   c) Select **L**ook Up . . . . **Alt**+**L**
   WordPerfect displays found words in first list box.
   To quickly select previously looked up words:

   a) Select H**i**story menu . . . . **Alt**+**I**

   b) Select desired word . . . . **↑↓**, **↵**

4. Select desired word in list box . . . . **Tab**, **↑↓**
   If necessary, press Tab until list box is selected.

5. Select **R**eplace . . . . **Alt**+**R**
   to replace word in document with selected word.

   OR   **OR**

   Select **C**lose . . . . **Alt**+**C**

268

Change Thesaurus Dictionary

Thesaurus dictionary files are named WP{WP}xx.THS, where xx represents the language of the file (for example: WP{WP}US.THS indicates U.S. English while, WP{WP}UK.THS indicates United Kingdom English).

1. Select **T**ools menu .... `Alt` + `T`

2. Select **T**hesaurus .... `T`

3. Select **D**ictionary menu .... `Alt` + `D`

4. Select **C**hange Dictionary .... `C`

5. Select filename in **F**iles list box .... `Alt` + `↓`, `¼`
   See DIRECTORIES — LOCATING FILES on page 25.

6. Select **Select** .... `↵`

7. Select **C**lose .... `Alt` + `C`

TYPEOVER/INSERT MODE

Changes keyboard entry mode between Typeover and Insert. Use Typeover mode when you want to replace existing characters to the right of the insertion point as you type. Switch back to Insert mode (the default mode) when you want text before insertion point to move as you type.

• Press **Insert** .... `Ins`
  to switch between Typeover and Insert mode.

  NOTE: *When "Typeover" appears in status bar, you are in Typeover mode; otherwise you are in Insert mode.*

TYPESETTING

Word Spacing

1. Place insertion point where new word spacing will begin.
2. Select Layout menu .... Alt + L
3. Select Typesetting .... N
4. Select one option in Word Spacing group:

   O Normal .... Alt + N
   spaces words according to printer
   specifications.

   O WordPerfect Optimal .... Alt + W
   spaces words according to WordPerfect
   specifications.

   O Percent of Optimal .... Alt + E
   sets spacing to a percentage of normal
   or a specified pitch.

   a) Select Percent of Optimal text box .... Tab
   b) Type percentage .... number
   OR   **OR**
   a) Select Set Pitch text box .... Tab
   b) Type pitch (characters per inch) .... number

5. Select OK .... ↵

TYPESETTING (continued)

Letter Spacing

1. Place insertion point where new letter spacing will begin.
2. Select Layout menu .... [Alt]+[L]
3. Select Typesetting .... [N]
4. Select one option in Letterspacing group:

   ○ Select Normal .... [Alt]+[M]
     spaces letters according to printer's
     specifications.

   ○ WordPerfect Optimal .... [Alt]+[O]
     spaces letters according to WordPerfect
     specifications.

   ○ Percent of Optimal .... [Alt]+[R]
     sets spacing to a percentage of normal
     or a specified pitch.

     a) Select Percent of Optimal text box .... [Tab]
     b) Type percentage .... **number**
     OR   **OR**
     a) Select Set Pitch text box .... [Tab]
     b) Type pitch (characters per inch) .... **number**

5. Select OK .... [↵]

Kern Text

See KERN TEXT on page 135.

Leading Adjustment

See LINE HEIGHT (LEADING) ADJUSTMENT on page 144.

Printer Commands

See Insert Printer Commands on page 194.

TYPESETTING (continued)

Word Spacing Limits in Full Justified Text

1. Place insertion point where new word spacing will begin.

2. Select <u>L</u>ayout menu .... `Alt`+`L`

3. Select Typesetti<u>n</u>g .... `N`

4. Select <u>C</u>ompressed To: (0% to 100%) text box .. `Alt`+`C`

5. Type percentage .... **number**
   *Percentage determines minimum amount that fully justified
   text can be compressed.*

6. Select E<u>x</u>panded To: (100% to Unlimited) text box `Alt`+`X`

7. Type percentage .... **number**
   *Percentage determines maximum amount that fully justified
   text can be expanded. A number over 1000% is considered unlimited.*

8. Select **OK** .... `↵`

Underline Spaces and Tabs

1. Place insertion point where new underline setting will begin.

2. Select <u>L</u>ayout menu .... `Alt`+`L`

3. Select Typesetti<u>n</u>g .... `N`

4. Select or clear ☐Underline <u>S</u>paces .... `Alt`+`S`

   AND/OR   **AND/OR**

   Select or clear ☐Underline <u>T</u>abs .... `Alt`+`T`

5. Select **OK** .... `↵`

Set First Baseline at Top Margin

*Sets baseline of first line of text consistently on top margin of every page.
This is especially useful when creating forms.*

1. Set line height to fixed (page 143).

2. Place insertion point at top of document.

3. Select <u>L</u>ayout menu .... `Alt`+`L`

4. Select Typesetti<u>n</u>g .... `N`

5. Select ☐<u>F</u>irst Baseline at Top Margin .... `Alt`+`F`

6. Select **OK** .... `↵`

UNDELETE

WordPerfect temporarily stores your last three deletions in memory. You can view or restore these deletions.

Restore Deletions

1. Place insertion point where deleted text will be restored.
2. Select **E**dit menu . . . . **Alt**+**E**
3. Select U**n**delete . . . . **N**
   Last deletion appears as selected text at insertion point.
4. If necessary, select **P**revious . . . . **P**
   until desired deletion appears.
5. Select **R**estore . . . . **R**

NOTE: Also see UNDO below.

UNDO

Reverses the last change made to a document, such as text you have typed, text you have deleted, or formats you have changed.

NOTE: Undo will not reverse insertion point movements, sorted text, conversion of tabular columns to tables, generated lists, or merged text.

1. Select **E**dit menu . . . . **Alt**+**E**
2. Select **U**ndo . . . . **U**

UNITS OF MEASURE

These options determine units of measure WordPerfect uses.

NOTE: In this book we have assumed inches as the unit of measure.

Set Default Unit of Measurement

1. Select File menu .... `Alt`+`F`

2. Select Preferences .... `E`

3. Select Display .... `D`

> **To set default units for dialog box entry and display:**
>
> • Open Display and
>   Entry of Numbers `[　　♦]` .... `Alt`+`E`, `F4`
>
>   and select desired unit of measure .... **character**
>   _Inches ("), inches (i), centimeters (c), points (p),_
>   _1200ths of an inch (w)_
>
> **To set default units displayed on status bar:**
>
> • Open Status Bar Display `[　　♦]` ... `Alt`+`B`, `F4`
>
>   and select desired unit of measure .... **character**
>   _Inches ("), inches (i), centimeters (c), points (p),_
>   _1200ths of an inch (w)_

4. Select OK .... `↵`

Enter Value In a Different Unit of Measure

With these steps you can specify a unit of measure — other than the default (see above) — when typing a measure in a text or increment box.

FROM A DIALOG BOX

1. Select increment or text box .... `Alt`+**letter**

2. Type value .... **number**

3. Type desired unit of measurement code .... **code**

   " or **i**   inches
   c   centimeters
   p   points
   w   1200ths of an inch

WordPerfect converts number entered to default unit of measure.

Example: Enter 72p (72 points) and WordPerfect will convert
number to one inch.

WIDOW/ORPHAN

Widow/Orphan protection prevents Widows (last line of a paragraph appearing alone at the top of a page) and Orphans (first line of a paragraph appearing alone at the bottom of a page) from occurring.

Turn Widow/Orphan Protection On/Off

1. Place insertion point at top of page where setting will begin.
2. Select Layout menu .... `Alt`+`L`
3. Select Page .... `P`
4. Select or deselect Widow/Orphan .... `W`

WORD AND LETTER SPACING

See TYPESETTING — Word Spacing on page 269.
See TYPESETTING — Letter Spacing on page 270.

WORD COUNT

Counts the number of words in current document or selected text.

1. If desired, select text to count.
2. Select Tools menu .... `Alt`+`T`
3. Select Word Count .... `W`
   WordPerfect displays number of words in current document or selected text.
4. Select OK .... `←`

WORDPERFECT CHARACTERS

Provides additional characters other than those found on the keyboard.

1. Place insertion point where WordPerfect character will be inserted.

2. Press **Ctrl + W** (WordPerfect Characters) . . . . . `Ctrl`+`W`

   OR   **OR**

   Select F**o**nt menu . . . . `Alt`+`O`

   - Select **W**P Characters . . . . `W`

   FROM WORDPERFECT CHARACTERS DIALOG BOX

   To select character from Characters list:

   a) Open **S**et `[    ▾]` . . . . `Alt`+`S`, `F4`

      and select desired character set . . . . **character**

      ASCII, Multinational 1, Multinational 2, Box Drawing,
      Typographic Symbols, Iconic Symbols, Math/Scientific,
      Math/Scientific Ext., Greek, Hebrew, Cyrillic,
      Japanese, User Defined

   b) Select character in **C**haracters list box `Alt`+`C`, `⬍`

   To select character by typing its assigned numbers:

   a) Select **N**umber text box . . . . `Alt`+`N`

   b) Type number (0-11) of character set . . . . **number**

   c) Press **,** (comma) . . . . `,`

   d) Type number of character in set . . . . **number**

   Example: 4,8

   NOTE: *In the Number text box, you can create*
   diacritics, digraphs and symbols (special
   character combinations) by typing each character
   without using a comma between them (i.e., vz).

3. Select **I**nsert . . . . `Alt`+`I`
   to insert character and leave dialog box open.

   OR   **OR**

   Select Insert **a**nd Close . . . . `Alt`+`A`
   to insert character and close dialog box.

ZOOM

Enlarges or condenses text or graphics display within document window. Also see Change Zoom Level using the Ruler on page 211.

1. Select <u>V</u>iew menu . . . . **Alt** + **V**
2. Select <u>Z</u>oom . . . . **Z**
3. Select one option . . . . **↑↓** , **↵**
   <u>5</u>0%, <u>7</u>5%, <u>1</u>00%, 15<u>0</u>%, <u>2</u>00%, To <u>P</u>age Width, <u>O</u>ther

   If <u>O</u>ther was selected,

   a) Type zoom percentage . . . . **number**
   b) Select **OK** . . . . **↵**

Adobe Type Manager (ATM) *WP5.2*

Adobe Type Manager is a Windows utility that displays PostScript Type 1 fonts on your screen and prints them on non-PostScript printers. You can use the fonts installed with ATM in your WordPerfect documents and other Windows applications. In WordPerfect, you will need to select a Windows printer driver to use these fonts.

NOTE: You can use both Adobe Type 1 and Windows TrueType fonts in the same document.

To Install Adobe Type Manager:

1. Select **File** menu from Program Manager.
2. Type `a:\install`

   OR

   Type `b:\install`
3. Follow prompts.

   Refer to your documentation for details.

To run ATM Control Panel:

• Select the ATM icon from Program Manager's Main group.

   ATM Control Panel options:

   • Turn ATM on or off.
   • Set the font cache size.
   • Set how ATM uses fonts.
   • Add or delete Type 1 fonts.

   Refer to your documentation for details.

Graphics Conversion Utility

The WordPerfect Graphics Conversion utility (GRAPHCNV.EXE) converts the following graphic formats into WordPerfect's WPG graphic file format: BMP, CGM, DHP, DXF, EPS, GEM, HPGL, IMG MSP, PCX, PIC, PNTG, PPIC, TIF, WMF, WPG. Under normal conditions most graphic files will convert to WPG graphic format automatically when retrieved into a WordPerfect graphics box; however, the Graphics Conversion Program is useful when converting multiple files or when you want WordPerfect to convert a graphic file in a specific way.

Convert graphic files with Graphics Conversion

1. Select **File** menu from Program Manager.

2. Select **Run**.

3. Type `c:\wpc\graphcnv`

4. Select **OK**.

5. Specify path and filename or filespec of file(s) to convert.

   Example: c:\art*.eps

   AND

   If necessary, specify a conversion switch.

   Example: c:\art*.eps /g=16
   See Graphics Conversion switches on next page.

6. Press **Enter**.

7. Specify directory for output file(s).

8. Press **Enter**.

Graphics Conversion Switches

The switches that follow, when added to the end of input file (step 5 on previous page), will customize the way the input file(s) convert.

/b=#	Sets the background color for the output file, where # represent one of the following colors: 1=black, 2=blue, 3=green, 4=cyan, 5=red, 6=magenta, 7=brown, 8=white. If this option is omitted, the background defaults to white.
/c=2	Converts colors of the input file to monochrome.
/c=16	Converts colors of the input file to the standard 16 color palette.
/c=265	Converts colors of the input file to the standard 256 color palette.
/c=b	Converts colors of the input file to black (can not be used with bitmap images).
/c=w	Converts colors of the input file to white (can not be used with bitmap images).
/f=#	Converts file that has been converted with the /c or /g option to change the fill color, where # represents one of the following colors: 1=black, 2=blue, 3=green, 4=cyan, 5=red, 6=magenta, 7=brown, 8=white.
/g=16	Converts colors of the input file to the standard 16 shades of the gray palette.
/g=256	Converts colors of the input file to 16 shades of gray.
/h	Displays help for Graphics Conversion Program.
/l	Sends conversion status messages for each file converted to the printer device.
/l=filename	Sends conversion status messages for each file converted to a specified file.
/m	Inverts monochrome bitmap images.
/n=#	After a color or gray scale conversion, use this option to change the line color, where # represents one of the following colors: 1=black, 2=blue, 3=green, 4=cyan, 5=red, 6=magenta, 7=brown, 8=white.

Macro Command Inserter *WP5.2*

The Macro Command Inserter utility helps you to insert macro and programming commands into a WordPerfect macro file. When editing a macro file (macro files can be opened like any other WordPerfect document), just press Ctrl + M and the Macro Command Inserter window will appear. You can then choose commands from the Commands list, instead of looking them up and typing them. The Token Edit text box will show the command and will prompt you for additional parameters the command may need. Finally, select the Insert button when the command is complete to place it into the macro file.

Macros

The macros that have been added or enhanced since WP 5.1 are shown in bold type. By default, these macros are located in the directory: **C:\WPWIN\MACROS**

Attribute	adds attribute while an attribute code is highlighted	ADD.WCM
Bar code	prints POSTNET bar code for zip code in text	**BARCODE.WCM**
Blank line	insert blank line before current line	INSERT.WCM
Bookmark	insert bookmark	MARK.WCM
Bookmark	find bookmarks created with MARK.WCM	FIND.WCM
Bullet	define bullet character for BULLET.WCM	**BULLETDF.WCM**
Bullet	insert bullet character with indent	**BULLET.WCM**
Calculate	recalculates formulas in a table	RECALC.WCM
Capitalize	first character of word	CAPITAL.WCM
Codes	takes you to edit screen of highlighted code	EDIT.WCM
Codes	create document representing codes of current document	CODES.WCM
Delete	text in current line	DELETE.WCM
Endnote	converts endnotes to footnotes	ENDFOOT.WCM
Envelope	prints envelope using address in document	**ENVELOPE.WCM**
Equation	create in-line equations placed in a user box list.	INLINE.WCM
Fonts	search and replace font attributes	REPLACE.WCM
Footnote	converts to endnotes	FOOTEND.WCM
Forms	create memos, letters, and other form types	**MEMO.WCM**
Glossary	edit or add terms used by GLOSSARY.WCM	GLOSEDIT.WCM
Glossary	create terms from abbreviations	GLOSSARY.WCM
Justify	select left, right, center, or full	JUSTIFY.WCM
Labels	select from a predefined list	LABELS.WCM
Line	go to specified line number	LINENUM.WCM
Paper	select a paper type	PAPER.WCM
Pleading	creates a style for pleading papers*	**PLEADING.WCM**
Quotes	substitutes curly quotes for straight quotes	**SMQUOTE.WCM**
Transpose	reverse order of the two characters preceding insertion point	TRANSPOSE.WCM

Mail Enabled *WP 5.2*

With Mail you can mail your current document or just the text you have
selected, to another work station without exiting WordPerfect for
Windows. This feature will only be available if a compatible E-mail
system (WP mail, VIM Mail, or MAPI Mail) was located by WordPerfect
when you installed WordPerfect for Windows 5.2. If you install a
compatible E-Mail system after installing WordPerfect for Windows 5.2,
you will have to update your WPC.INI file as described below.

To add Mail feature to WordPerfect for Windows Version 5.2:

1. Run Notepad from Program Manager.
2. Select **File** menu.
3. Select **Open**.
4. Type `wpc.ini`
5. Select **OK**.

   If you have a MAPI compatible Mail system,

   insert the following section below the [App Server] section:

   ```
   [Mail]
   MAPI=&Mail
   ```

   If you have a VIM compatible Mail system,

   insert the following section below the [App Server] section:

   ```
   [Mail]
   VIM=&Mail
   ```
6. Select **File** menu.
7. Select **Save**.

Mail Enabled (continued)

To mail all or part of a document:

1. If desired, select part of document to mail.

2. Select **File** menu from WordPerfect.

3. Select **Mail**.

4. Follow prompts for your Mail system.

Spell Utility

You can use the WordPerfect Spell utility (SPELL.EXE) to manage the dictionaries WordPerfect uses to check your documents.

To Manage Speller Dictionaries:

1. Select **File** menu from Program Manager.

2. Select **Run**.

3. Type `c:\wpc\spell` or `c:\wpwin\spell`

4. Select **OK**

5. Select desired option from menu.

6. When done, select **O** (Exit).

CUA/WP DOS 5.1 Keystrokes

ACTION	CUA	WP5.1 DOS
Bold	CTRL+B	CTRL+B or F6
Cancel	ESC	ESC
Cancel Merge	CTRL+BREAK	CTRL+BREAK
Center	SHIFT+F7	SHIFT+F6
Center with Dot Leader	SHIFT+F7, SHIFT+F7	SHIFT+F6, SHIFT+F6
Clear Document	CTRL+SHIFT+F4	CTRL+SHIFT+F7
Close Document	CTRL+F4	F7
Column, Start New	CTRL+ENTER	CTRL+ENTER
Columns	ALT+SHIFT+F9	ALT+F7, C
Control Menu, Application	ALT+SPACEBAR	ALT+SPACEBAR
Control Menu, Document	ALT+HYPHEN (-)	ALT+HYPHEN (-)
Copy	CTRL+C	CTRL+C
Copy Active Window to Clipboard	ALT+PRINT SCREEN	ALT+PRINT SCREEN
Copy Screen to Clipboard	PRINT SCREEN	PRINT SCREEN
Cut	CTRL+X	CTRL+X
Date Code	CTRL+SHIFT+F5	SHIFT+F5, D, C
Date Text	CTRL+F5	SHIFT+F5, D, T
Define menu	SHIFT+F12	-----
Delete Characters/Selection	BKSPACE/DELETE	BKSPACE/DELETE
Delete to Beginning of Word	-----	HOME, BKSPACE
Delete to End of Line	CTRL+DEL	CTRL+END
Delete to End of Page	CTRL+SHIFT+DELETE	CTRL+PGDN
Delete word	CTRL+BKSPACE	CTRL+BKSPACE or CTRL+DEL
Document menu (Layout)	CTRL+SHIFT+F9	SHIFT+F8, D
Draft Mode	CTRL+SHIFT+F3	CTRL+SHIFT+F3
Exit Application	ALT+F4	-----
Figure Edit	F11	ALT+F9, F, E
Figure Retrieve	F11	ALT+F9, F, R
File Manager (List Files)	-----	F5
Flush Right	ALT+F7	ALT+F6
Flush Right with Dot leader	ALT+F7, ALT+F7	ALT+F6, ALT+F6
Font	F9	CTRL+F8
Font Size	CTRL+S	CTRL+S
Footnote	-----	CTRL+F7
Generate	ALT+F12	ALT+SHIFT+F5
Go To	CTRL+G	CTRL+G
Hard Page	CTRL+ENTER	CTRL+ENTER
Hard Return	ENTER	ENTER
Hard Return, in an Outline	SHIFT+ENTER	SHIFT+ENTER
Help	F1	F1
Help, What Is?	SHIFT+F1	-----
Horizontal Line	CTRL+F11	ALT+F9, L, H
Hyphen, Hard	CTRL+-	HOME, -
Hyphen, Soft	CTRL+-	CTRL+-
Hyphenation Code, Cancel	CTRL+/	CTRL+/

ACTION	CUA	WP5.1 DOS
Indent	F7	F4
Indent, Double	CTRL+SHIFT+F7	SHIFT+F4
Indent, Hanging	CTRL+F7	F4, SHIFT+TAB
Insert/Typeover mode	INSERT	INSERT
Italic	CTRL+I	CTRL+I
Justify Center	CTRL+J	CTRL+J
Justify Full	CTRL+F	CTRL+F
Justify Left	CTRL+L	CTRL+L
Justify Right	CTRL+R	CTRL+R
Line menu (Layout)	SHIFT+F9	SHIFT+F8, L
Line Draw	CTRL+D	CTRL+D
Macro Play	ALT+F10	ALT+F10
Macro Record	CTRL+F10	CTRL+F10
Macro Stop	CTRL+SHIFT+F10	CTRL+SHIFT+F10
Margin Release	SHIFT+TAB	SHIFT+TAB
Margin Release, in a Table	CTRL+SHIFT+TAB	CTRL+SHIFT+TAB
Margins	CTRL+F8	SHIFT+F8, M
Mark Text	F12	ALT+F5
Mark Text Define	SHIFT+F12	CTRL+F9, F
Menu bar	F10 or ALT	ALT
Menu, back one level	ESC	ESC
Merge Codes menu	CTRL+F12, C	SHIFT+F9
Merge menu	CTRL+F12	CTRL+F9, M
Merge/Sort	CTRL+SHIFT+F12	CTRL+F9
Merge End of Field	ALT+ENTER	ALT+ENTER or F9
Merge End of Record	ALT+SHIFT+ENTER	ALT+SHIFT+ENTER
New File	SHIFT+F4	-----
Next Application	ALT+TAB	ALT+TAB
Next Cell in Table	TAB	TAB
Next Document	CTRL+F6	SHIFT+F3
Next Level of Outline	TAB	TAB
Next Pane	F6	CTRL+F1
Next Window	ALT+F6	ALT+SHIFT+F6
Normal	CTRL+N	CTRL+N
Open File	F4	SHIFT+F10
Page menu (Layout)	ALT+F9	SHIFT+F8, P
Paragraph Define	ALT+SHIFT+F5	SHIFT+F5, O, D
Paragraph Number	ALT+F5	SHIFT+F5, O, P
Paragraph Menu (Layout)	-----	SHIFT+F8, P
Paste	CTRL+V	CTRL+V
Preferences (Setup)	CTRL+SHIFT+F1	SHIFT+F1
Previous Application	ALT+SHIFT+TAB	ALT+SHIFT+TAB
Previous Cell in Table	SHIFT+TAB	SHIFT+TAB
Previous Document	CTRL+SHIFT+F6	ALT+SHIFT+F3
Previous Outline Level	SHIFT+TAB	SHIFT+TAB
Previous Pane	SHIFT+F6	CTRL+SHIFT+F1

ACTION	CUA	WP5.1 DOS
Print	F5	SHIFT+F7
Print Current Document	CTRL+P	CTRL+P
Print Preview	SHIFT+F5	ALT+SHIFT+F7
Redisplay Screen	CTRL+F3	CTRL+F3
Replace	CTRL+F2	ALT+F2
Reveal Codes	ALT+F3	F11 or ALT+F3
Ruler	ALT+SHIFT+F3	SHIFT+F3
Save	SHIFT+F3	-----
Save As	F3	F10
Search	F2	F2
Search Next	SHIFT+F2	SHIFT+F2
Search Previous	ALT+F2	ALT+SHIFT+F2
Select (Block)	F8	F12 or ALT+F4
Select Cell (Table Block)	SHIFT+F8	SHIFT+F12
Select Paragraph	-----	CTLR+SHIFT+F4
Select Sentence	-----	CTRL+F4
Sort	CTRL+SHIFT+F12	CTRL+F9, R
Space, Hard	CTRL+SPACE	CTRL+SPACE
Special Codes	ALT+SHIFT+F8	ALT+SHIFT+F8
Speller	CTRL+F1	CTRL+F2
Styles	ALT+F8	ALT+F8
Tab, Decimal	ALT+SHIFT+F7	CTRL+F6
Tab, Hard Center	SHIFT+F9, O, C	HOME, SHIFT+F6
Tab, Hard Center with Dot Leader	SHIFT+F9, O, N	HOME, HOME, SHIFT+F6
Tab, Hard Decimal	ALT+SHIFT+F7	HOME, CTRL+F6
Tab, Hard Decimal with Dot Leader	SHIFT+F9, O, M	HOME, HOME, CTRL+F6
Tab, Hard Left	SHIFT+F9, O, L	HOME, TAB
Tab, Hard Left with Dot Leader	SHIFT+F9, O, E	HOME, HOME, TAB
Tab, Hard Right	SHIFT+F9, O, R	HOME, ALT+F6
Tab, Hard Right with Dot Leader	SHIFT+F9, O, T	HOME, HOME, ALT+F6
Tab, in a Table	CTRL+TAB	CTRL+TAB
Table, Append Row	ALT+SHIFT+INSERT	ALT+SHIFT+INSERT
Table, Delete Row	ALT+DELETE	ALT+DELETE
Table, Hard Row	CTRL+ENTER	CTRL+ENTER
Table, Insert Row	ALT+INSERT	ALT+INSERT
Tables	CTRL+F9	ALT+F7, T
Text Box, Create	ALT+F11	ALT+F9, B, C
Text Box, Edit	ALT+SHIFT+F11	ALT+F9, B, E
Thesaurus	ALT+F1	ALT+F1
Undelete	ALT+SHIFT+BKSPACE	F3
Underline	CTRL+U	CTRL+U or F8
Undo	ALT+BKSPACE or CTRL+Z	CTRL+Z
Vertical Line	CTRL+SHIFT+F11	ALT+F9, L, V
WP Characters	CTRL+W	CTRL+W

286

INDEX

INDEX

287

288

INDEX

INDEX

289

INDEX

INDEX